Medical Ethics

Look for these and other books in the Lucent Overview Series:

Abortion
Adoption
Advertising
AIDS
Alcoholism
Animal Rights
The Beginning of Writing
The Brain
Cancer
Censorship
Child Abuse
Children's Rights
Cities
Civil Liberties
Cloning
The Collapse of the Soviet Union
Cults
Dealing with Death
Death Penalty
Democracy
Depression
Diabetes
Drug Abuse
Drugs and Sports
Drug Trafficking
Eating Disorders
Elections
Endangered Species
The End of Apartheid in South Africa
Energy Alternatives
Environmental Groups
Epidemics
Espionage
Ethnic Violence
Euthanasia
Gangs
Gay Rights

Gun Control
Hate Groups
Hazardous Waste
Health Care
Homeless Children
Homelessness
The Internet
Juvenile Crime
Medical Ethics
Memory
Mental Illness
Militias
Money
Obesity
Oil Spills
The Olympic Games
Ozone
The Palestinian-Israeli Accord
Paranormal Phenomena
Pesticides
Police Brutality
Population
Poverty
The Rebuilding of Bosnia
Schools
School Violence
Sexual Harrassment
Smoking
Space Exploration
Sports in America
Suicide
The U.S. Congress
The U.S. Presidency
Violence Against Women
Women's Rights
Zoos

Medical Ethics

by Debbie Levy

Lucent
Books

Library of Congress Cataloging-in-Publication Data

Levy, Debbie.
    Medical ethics / by Debbie Levy.
        p. cm. — (Lucent overview series)
    Includes bibliographical references (p.) and index.
      ISBN 1-56006-547-8 (lib.: alk. paper)
      1. Medical ethics—Juvenile literature.   [1. Medical ethics.]   I.
    Title.   II. Series.
      R724 .L458   2001
      174'.2—dc21

                                        00-009708

Copyright © 2001 by Lucent Books, Inc.
P.O. Box 289011, San Diego, CA 92198-9011
Printed in the U.S.A.

Contents

Introduction

A BABY GIRL is born in Boston, nearly dead as she enters the world. While still in her mother's womb, she has suffered severe asphyxia, or lack of oxygen. As a result, the baby—called Baby L. in press reports—is born severely underdeveloped. She stays in the hospital for fourteen months. After she goes home, Baby L. must return to the hospital many times to be treated for pneumonia and infections. Her heart stops four times and must be resuscitated, or started again. She frequently requires artificial means—a respirator—to breathe. For the first two years of her life, Baby L. never functions beyond the level of a two- to four-month-old.

Each time Baby L. requires treatment, her mother requests that doctors do everything possible to help her. By the time she is two years old, however, her doctors believe that continuing treatment is not in Baby L.'s best interest. They feel so strongly about this that they go to court, where they argue that the use of mechanical means to keep the baby breathing is "futile and inhumane"[1] because it will not help improve Baby L.'s underlying medical problems.

In Maine, another child, a four-year-old boy, is very sick. He is infected with HIV, the human immunodeficiency virus, which causes AIDS. In this case, it is the boy's mother who wants to discontinue treatment. Her three-year-old daughter has recently died from AIDS, and this mother believes that her daughter suffered unnecessarily as a result of the medical treatment she received. The Maine Department of Human Services strongly disagrees with the mother's choice, calling it child neglect and abuse. The department goes to court to seek custody of the boy.

Who was right in these two disputes? None of the adults involved sought to injure the two sick children. Each of them reached conclusions based on values, or principles, that most people would agree are good: doing no harm, trying to improve health, reducing suffering, protecting vulnerable individuals. Yet the disagreements in both cases were so intense that they ended up in court.

What made these situations so difficult was that no one was clearly right or wrong. That is also what makes them

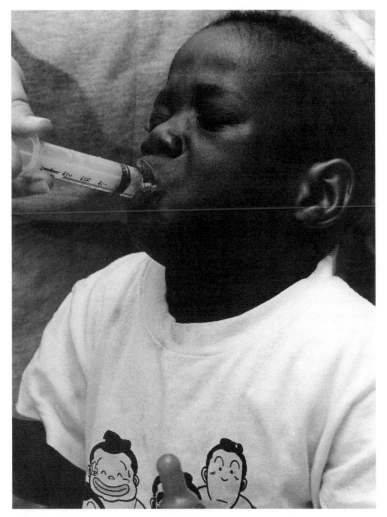

There are no clear-cut answers to difficult ethical questions such as whether to discontinue AIDS treatment for children whose parents do not want them to suffer unnecessarily.

apt introductions to a discussion of medical ethics. Medical ethics are the principles and values that apply when people face questions of morality in medical care. And although morality is about the choice of right over wrong, usually there is no absolutely clear right or wrong choice in ethical dilemmas. As the cases of Baby L. and the Maine HIV patient show, more than one value usually applies. To make matters more difficult, these values often conflict with one another. Complicating things further, different people often assert conflicting claims that they have the right to make decisions about which values should prevail.

Tangled web?

Conflicting choices, conflicting values, conflicting claims by would-be decision makers—all these may make medical ethics sound like a tangled web. In fact, although medical ethics can be complicated, they actually serve to untangle knotty problems in medical care. The values that make up medical ethics are not obscure or hard to understand, because they are simply the values that are widely viewed in society as defining good behavior. The process of applying medical ethics in particular cases involves identifying the values at issue and sorting through them to reach a resolution. It is not a scientific process. It is not a perfect process. But as a means of analyzing vexing and emotional medical situations, the process of applying medical ethics is central to the practice of medicine today.

Medical ethics are not formulated and handed down from on high. There is no fixed list of ethics that doctors, patients, and others must apply when moral questions arise in health care. Rather, the values that make up medical ethics come from many sources. Those sources go back as far as the fifth century B.C. to the principles stated in the Hippocratic oath, which doctors still follow today—including the well-known principle "First, do no harm." Current sources of medical ethics include religion and law, as well as the opinions of scholars, doctors, judges, and others.

Today, some of the most important general principles of medical ethics are the following:

• *beneficence*, the duty of doctors to work in the best interests of their patients. Part of beneficence is maximizing possible benefits and minimizing possible harms.

• *do no harm*, the obligation of doctors to take no action harmful to their patients.

• *autonomy or self-determination*, respect by doctors for the individuality of their patients. This includes the right of patients to care that is tailored to their individual circumstances as well as the right to make their own decisions. Where a patient is not competent to make his or her own decisions, as in the case of a young child or a person in a coma, autonomy sometimes refers to the right of a relative to make decisions on the patient's behalf.

• *justice*, fairness in how doctors treat their patients. This includes questions of fairness that arise when patients with similar health problems receive different treatments.

• *truthfulness*, the duty of doctors to inform patients truthfully of the facts concerning their condition.

• *confidentiality*, the obligation of doctors to maintain the privacy of their patients' personal information.

People who think about moral values in general are called ethicists; people who interpret and apply medical ethics are called medical ethicists or bioethicists. Medical

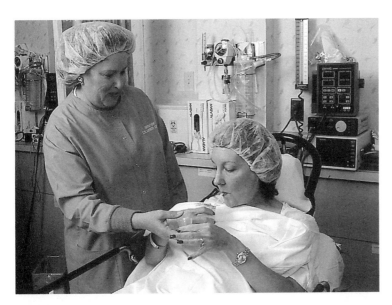

One of the main principles of medical ethics is beneficence, the duty of doctors to work in the best interests of their patients.

ethicists may be academic scholars, or they may work for hospitals or similar institutions. Ethicists may draft codes of ethics for certain groups of health care professionals to follow, such as the employees of a particular hospital. They may write articles or propose rules that reflect ethical principles. One group that issues opinions on specific medical ethical problems, for example, is the Council on Ethical and Judicial Affairs of the American Medical Association (AMA), a membership organization for physicians in the United States. But it is important to remember that medical ethicists do not create medical ethics, which come from many different sources and forces in society.

Setting priorities

Just as there is no master list of ethical principles, there is no list that firmly establishes which principle takes priority when two or more conflict. In the Baby L. case, the child's doctors believed that continued treatment was futile, violating the principle of "do no harm." They wanted this principle to take precedence over the mother's right to make decisions for her baby. In the Maine case, the boy's mother believed that treatment for her son's HIV infection would violate the "do no harm" principle, as well as the principle of autonomy that supports a patient's right to make decisions. The state Department of Human Services sought to override her arguments with its own assertion of "do no harm," in addition to claims based on the principle of beneficence. In both cases, the question came down to this: Which principle should prevail?

There is no easy answer. In many, if not most, cases, no single ethical value clearly wins out over others. Instead, doctors, patients, judges, and others involved in ethical dilemmas must consider the competing principles in the case at hand and work out the best resolution they can, taking into account all the circumstances.

In the case of the boy with HIV, a state court sided with the mother. "The state of Maine is now in no position to tell her [the mother], in the case of her unique experience, that she is wrong in her current judgment to wait for better and more reliable treatment methods,"[2] the judge said. In the Baby L. case, the court found a way out of making a difficult choice between the doctors' and the mother's ethical claims: it found a different doctor who agreed to treat the then two-year-old girl. Baby L. was transferred to that doctor's hospital. She was weaned from her respirator so that she could breathe on her own and was cured of pneumonia. Two years later, Baby L. was living at home with her family.

1

Experimental
Treatments

LITTLE MORE THAN one hundred years ago, medicine meant crude and dangerous practices: draining blood from the body in an effort to rid a person of disease, amputation, doses of addictive morphine to kill pain. These methods were often ineffective at best and deadly at worst. Medicine was powerless to stop many from dying of childhood diseases, such as scarlet fever and whooping cough. The influenza, or flu, epidemic of 1918 killed 675,000 Americans and more than 21 million people worldwide in just a few months.

Today, vaccines have all but wiped out many once-common diseases. Medicines effectively treat people who fall ill from a wide variety of infections and other illnesses—and who would have died from those illnesses fifty or one hundred years ago. Doctors today know how to perform lifesaving surgery that was unheard of in the not-so-distant past. Progress in medical science in the past century has been stunning, indeed, and it marches on, with research and experiments funded by both government agencies and private companies.

This forward march in medical progress takes place on a path crowded with patients awaiting treatments for their ailments. Thousands of research experiments, also called clinical trials, begin every year. One major research center alone, such as the Duke University Medical Center in Durham, North Carolina, can have two thousand medical experiments involving human subjects going on at a time. Duke's medical experiments annually receive millions of dollars in federal government funds, and attract more than 1 million patients every year from all over the world.

Researchers and drug companies need these patients as research subjects in testing their new and evolving treatments. People who participate in research studies contribute a great service to society by helping scientists weed out ineffective or dangerous treatments and promote successful ones. They may also help themselves, depending on the success of the experiments in question.

Often, however, the patients who are candidates for medical research are desperately sick. They will grasp at any chance to get better, even a practice that is unproved and risky. The very characteristics that make them obvious targets as research subjects also lead to serious ethical issues, for such patients are vulnerable to those who hold out hope

Vaccines have nearly eliminated once-deadly diseases such as influenza.

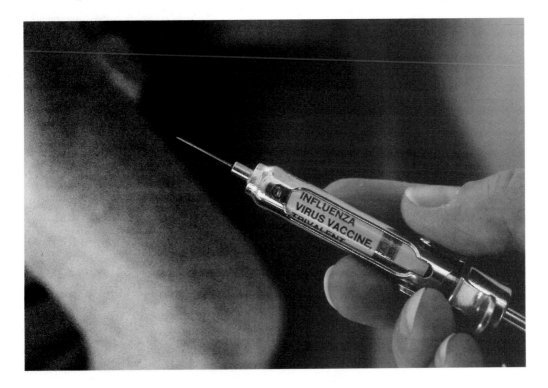

and susceptible to pressures concerning experimental treatments. The main ethical dilemma of experimental treatments is how to balance the desire of scientists and society to develop new treatments against the interests of patients who—however desperate they are for a cure—deserve to be treated with care and exposed to the least amount of risk possible.

Tragic history

More than one million patients a year from all over the world participate in experimental treatments at Duke University Medical Center in Durham, North Carolina.

Most of the medical community's ideas about protecting patients in medical research grew out of tragic experience with studies that abused their human subjects during the twentieth century. The first of these was the so-called Tuskegee study. In 1932, the United States Public Health Service, a government agency, began a study involving hundreds of African American men from Tuskegee, Alabama. These men, who lived in poverty, suffered from syphilis, a sexually transmitted disease. Researchers told the men that

Although penicillin, a drug found to cure syphilis, became available to the public in the 1940s, syphilis patients in the Tuskegee study were denied the product.

they would receive treatment, but, in fact, treatment was never the purpose of the study. Instead, researchers intended to study the course of the disease over a period of years to see how it affected those who had it.

The Tuskegee study ran for forty years, and during that time the men were never told the truth. They were given placebos, which are nonmedical substances made to look like medicine. Even when the drug penicillin—which was found to cure syphilis—became available in the late 1940s, it was not offered to the men in the study, who continued receiving placebos.

Ironically, this cruel treatment yielded rich scientific results that helped doctors understand and treat syphilis. Similarly, medical science learned more about disorders of the brain on the basis of the results of experiments performed by Nazi physicians on their captives during World War II. During the cold war, American scientists injected plutonium into patients to learn how the body responds to radioactivity. Again, society benefited from these practices, at least in a narrow sense: Scientific knowledge useful to the public at large was expanded. But in each of these cases, the gain in medical knowledge was obtained at moral costs that nearly everyone today would deem unacceptable. First,

Unethical research by Nazi physicians included this test in which a prisoner's response to prolonged exposure to cold is observed in order to gather information about hypothermia.

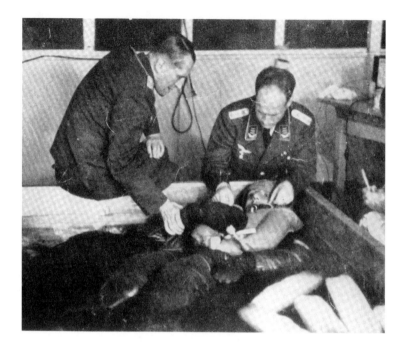

the research subjects had no real choice in deciding whether or not to serve as research subjects. Second, the risks these people were exposed to were simply too severe.

The growing understanding that some types of research are by their nature inhumane and that medical experiments are unacceptable when conducted on people who are not given a true choice about being research subjects led to two international agreements that today govern medical research on human subjects. The first was the Nuremberg Code, adopted in 1947. The Nuremberg Code was written by the U.S. judges who presided at the postwar trials of Nazi doctors accused of war crimes for their role in unethical experiments. The second international document was the Declaration of Helsinki, adopted in 1964 and revised several times since then.

Both of these legal codes emphasize that the rights of individual patients or research subjects have priority over scientific and societal goals. Both also focus on the importance of patient autonomy, especially the right of an individual to make informed decisions about his or her own fate. As the Declaration of Helsinki states:

Every biomedical research project involving human subjects should be preceded by careful assessment of predictable risks in comparison with foreseeable benefits to the subject or to others. Concern for the interests of the subject must always prevail over the interests of science and society.[3]

At the heart of the Nuremberg and Helsinki rules is the principle that no amount of scientific progress is worth the harm that is done when research subjects are treated without regard for their value as individuals.

Old lessons, new problems

Despite the lessons learned from the Tuskegee experiment and others and the widespread acceptance of the Nuremberg and Helsinki principles, the world of medical research is once again being stirred up with ethical concerns. In May 1999, the federal government forced Duke University to shut down all experiments on human subjects temporarily because of ethics violations. Among other things, the government said, Duke researchers failed to advise some patients of the purpose, risks, and benefits of the experiments in which they were participating. Gary Ellis, a federal official, explained, "Our concern was for the people in experiments facing risks they didn't know about or understand."[4]

Duke is far from the only research institution whose conduct of medical experiments has come under fire for ethical lapses. In 1999, for example, the federal Food and Drug Administration (FDA), another government agency, found that nearly 150 research firms had had ethical problems in their conduct of experiments on human subjects. In one experiment, researchers failed to tell patients that the treatment could leave them blind. And when the National Cancer Institute, part of the federal government's National Institutes of Health, reviewed its own clinical trials from 1995 to 1999, it found ethical problems in one-third of the cases.

What happened to Elyse MacEwen illustrates some of the most serious ethical problems that can arise in medical research today. According to the magazine *U.S. News & World Report,* when two-year-old Elyse was diagnosed with a rare childhood cancer, her parents went to the University of California, San Francisco. Doctors there said that Elyse could undergo major surgery to remove her bladder, reproductive organs, and surrounding tissue, followed by chemotherapy. But the doctors also offered another, seemingly more attractive option: They would give Elyse a combination of powerful new drugs, which they described as the most up-to-date treatment available. With these drugs, surgery was unnecessary.

The MacEwens agreed to the new drug regimen, and Elyse underwent a three-day course of drug treatment. Only afterward did the doctors present the MacEwens with a form that revealed that the treatment had not yet been approved by the FDA. Then the MacEwens learned that the standard treatment of surgery and chemotherapy was almost always successful. Elyse died, and the doctors failed to report her death to their supervisors at the university.

The federal official who ultimately investigated Elyse's treatment and death concluded that researchers violated medical ethics in at least four ways: They did not tell the MacEwens about the purpose or the risks of their research, they did not tell them the drugs were experimental, they failed to inform the MacEwens that the standard treatment would probably save their daughter, and they did not report Elyse's death to research overseers at the university. "It's tragic," the federal investigator, J. Thomas Puglisi, told a reporter in 1999. "It's very clear to me that the parents didn't understand the great risk of the research and the success rate of the standard treatment."[5]

Research safeguards

Safeguards do exist to help prevent the unethical treatment of patients in medical experiments. All research that is supported by a U.S. government agency must comply with regulations aimed at protecting human subjects. This policy covers much medical research undertaken today. The Office for Human Research Protections (OHRP) has primary responsibility for developing and implementing these protective policies. It has formal agreements with more than four

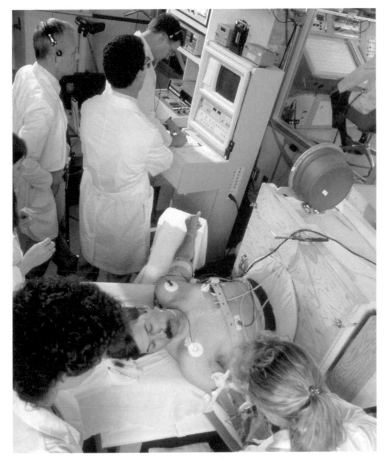

Technicians must comply with regulations aimed at protecting research volunteers when conducting tests such as this one, in which the effects of weightlessness are being studied.

thousand government-funded universities, hospitals, and other institutions that promise to follow procedures designed to ensure that they conduct research ethically.

Another government agency with a role in ensuring ethics in medical research is the National Bioethics Advisory Commission. The commission's function is to provide advice and recommendations on ethical issues arising from research on human subjects. The federal Food and Drug Administration also has a major role in research ethics. The FDA is responsible for regulating all research on new drugs and medical devices.

In all research trials, whether of experimental drugs and devices or new procedures, U.S. regulations rely heavily on two mechanisms to ensure that experiments are ethical:

informed consent and supervision of experiments by institutional review boards.

The idea behind informed consent is deceptively simple: For a person to agree, or consent, in a meaningful way to participate in a medical test, he or she must have sufficient knowledge of the experiment and its risks and benefits. Then, with a full understanding of the risks and benefits, the individual can make an informed decision about whether or not to participate. Informed consent serves the principle of individual autonomy by leaving decision making in the hands of the individual patient and ensuring that the patient is given the information necessary to make a meaningful choice.

Informed consent may boil down to a piece of paper—a standardized consent form—that a doctor gives a patient and the patient signs, but it is meant to be more than that. According to Gary Ellis, former director of the federal government's OHRP, informed consent is a dialogue between researcher and patient:

Doctors must inform their patients of an experiment's risks and benefits before the experiment begins.

Informed consent must be an ongoing, dynamic process, as new information becomes available or is desired. The informed consent document, or form, is one component—the written component—of the informed consent process. Federal regulations specify eight required elements of information (and six more optional elements of information) that must be conveyed to prospective subjects.[6]

Institutional review boards, or IRBs, form the second pillar on which the ethical structure of medical research rests. IRBs are local committees, and they include doctors and scientists from the research institution engaging in medical experimentation, as well as people who are not part of the scientific community. These boards review research protocols, or plans, for proposed studies. With the principle of minimal risk to the patient in mind, they may recommend changes in proposed experiments or reject them. IRBs also review informed consent procedures and continue monitoring experiments once they are under way.

Incomplete protections

Unfortunately, the protections that informed consent and IRBs are supposed to provide sometimes fall short. Problems begin with the IRB system. In 1998, the U.S. Department of Health and Human Services' Office of the Inspector General found that "IRBs across the country are inundated with protocols" and that this "increased workload coupled with resource constraints, causes problems for IRBs and threatens the adequacy of their reviews."[7] A 1996 report by the U.S. General Accounting Office stated, "In some cases the sheer number of studies necessitates that IRBs spend only 1 or 2 minutes of review per study."[8]

Sometimes IRBs themselves create ethical problems. According to the Office for Human Research Protections at Duke University, where human subject research was shut down in May 1999, two members of the IRB had conflicts of interest that affected their ability to review experiments neutrally. Both members worked for the university's Office of Grants and Contracts, which meant they were in charge of attracting federal research money to the school. In this capacity, these two officials had a vested interest in seeing that experiments get approved so that millions of dollars in research money would keep flowing in.

The informed consent system also suffers from ethical shortcomings. The world of medical research is competitive. Researchers who find new treatments and cures gain prestige and money, whether they work in private companies, in academic settings, or in government institutions. Researchers want to attract subjects, not scare them away with long, detailed explanations of all the things that could go wrong in an experiment. Sometimes this desire to attract patients results in consent forms that leave out more than they include or conversations between researchers and patients in which options other than the experimental treatment in question are skimmed over.

Informed consent is difficult to monitor because the process takes place behind closed doors, in private conversations between patients and researchers. "The discussion with the physician isn't taped," Dr. Henry Friedman of Duke University said in a 1999 interview. "The doctor says, 'I know there are other options, but there's nothing else out there that's right for you.' I am told all the time by patients that their physician didn't tell them about other options."[9]

Gene therapy crisis

The shortcomings and complexities of existing protections for human subjects in experimental treatments came to a head in late 1999 and 2000, when public attention focused on reports of deaths of patients in gene therapy studies. Genes are the chemical components in cells that contain instructions for the functions and processes of the human body. Mutated, or changed, genes that are defective can send out the wrong instructions, resulting in disease. Gene therapy is an experimental treatment that attempts to repair or replace harmful mutated genes in sick patients by transferring normal genes into the body.

Gene therapy has generally relied on specially altered viruses to carry the "good" genes into the body, because viruses are known to be good at burrowing into cells. Usually, viruses make people sick, but in gene therapy, scien-

tists attempt to disarm viruses by removing their harmful qualities and adding helpful genes aimed at the targeted disease. The altered virus, called a carrier or vector, is injected into patients with the expectation that it will deliver the helpful genes to the patients' cells. Unfortunately, the body's immune system is likely to fight off the carrier, even though it is harmless, and this tendency can lead to problems.

Public concern over gene therapy experiments began in September 1999, when eighteen-year-old Jesse Gelsinger of Arizona died while participating in such an experiment. Gelsinger had ornithine transcarbamylase (OTC) deficiency, a rare genetic disorder that mostly affects boys. If a person has a defective OTC gene, his or her body is unable to process ammonia, which is a normal by-product of the body's physical and chemical processes, known as metabolism. This inability often causes death soon after birth.

Gelsinger was born with a mild form of the disease and it was under control with drugs and a strict nonprotein diet. But

Genetic research helps gene therapists in their attempts to repair or replace harmful mutated genes in sick patients.

he volunteered to participate in an experiment conducted by the Institute for Human Gene Therapy at the University of Pennsylvania in Philadelphia. He hoped the research might lead to a cure that would help him and younger children with more serious forms of OTC deficiency.

The experimental treatment involved the infusion of trillions of genetically altered viruses into Gelsinger, the highest dose allowed under a research protocol that had been approved by the university's IRB and by the FDA. Unfortunately the treatment caused his liver to fail and his blood to thicken like jelly, clogging key blood vessels. One by one, his kidney, brain, and other organs shut down. Four days after Gelsinger received his treatment, he died.

Troubling issues

After Gelsinger's death, several troubling issues became public. First, unlike most gene therapy studies, which involve desperately sick patients who had conventional treatments that failed, the Pennsylvania experiment included relatively healthy patients, such as Jesse Gelsinger, who had responded well to existing treatments.

Second, two months after Gelsinger's death, the *Washington Post* reported that the irreversible and fatal blood reaction that the young man suffered had shown up earlier, when researchers at the University of Pennsylvania tested the gene treatment on monkeys. The researchers had moved forward with the human experiment despite the monkey deaths and despite criticism from some other scientists who thought the experiment was too risky. However, as the *Post*'s reporters noted, this did not necessarily mean that the researchers were reckless: "[E]xperimental therapies by definition often are dangerous, and the distinction between laudable perseverance and unjustifiable risk-taking can be blurry."[10]

But other conduct raised additional ethical concerns. For example, although the original consent form in the OTC experiment revealed that monkeys had died from a related experimental treatment, the final version that was given to patients failed to mention this. As Princeton University geneticist Leon Rosenberg commented, "If Gelsinger was never told that four people before him had Grade 3 [serious] toxicities [as a result of the treatment] and that monkeys had been killed by this kind of treatment, then you have to ask, did he really give informed consent or did he just give consent?"[11] At a U.S. Senate hearing in February 2000, Paul Gelsinger, Jesse's father, said he believed he and his son did not exercise truly informed consent.

Paul Gelsinger also wondered aloud at the hearing whether financial considerations caused researchers to play fast and loose with his son's well-being. Developing a gene therapy product could have brought the researchers not only prestige but also financial reward, through the research team's connection to a corporation with an interest in the study's results. "Guys want to own this [gene therapy cures] . . . they want to have the patents on it," Gelsinger said at the Senate hearing. "I thought this was all about people. I'm very disappointed to find that it is not all about people."[12]

In the wake of revelations about the experiment that led to Jesse Gelsinger's death, other gene therapy experiments were shut down in 2000, either by government order or by the research institutions themselves. In March 2000, the federal government tightened rules to protect patients in

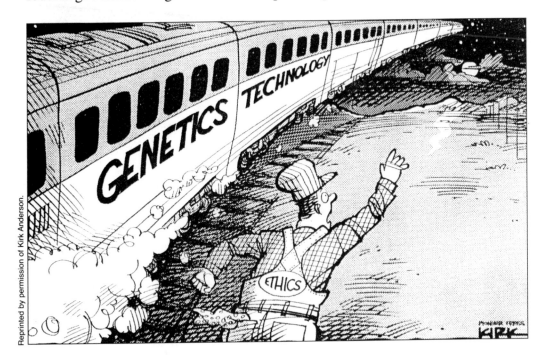

gene therapy experiments. Among other changes, university or corporate sponsors of experiments now have to hire specially trained people whose job is to ensure that patients' rights are protected and that studies are carried out according to the conditions set forth in the government approvals. As part of the new effort to protect patients in gene therapy experiments, the federal government announced that it will sponsor meetings four times a year where researchers can share information, including safety reports, from their studies.

Some critics remained skeptical. "This little idea that we're going to have a seminar a few times a year is not going to cut it," said ethicist George Annas of Boston University's School of Public Health.[13] He and some other ethicists, as well as scientists, want gene therapy experiments halted until scientific and ethical problems are better understood.

Some critics argue that gene therapy experiments should be discontinued until scientific and ethical problems are better understood.

A right to take risks

While critics say that the government and researchers have not gone far enough to protect patients in medical research trials, some patients fear that limits on experimental treatments in the name of ethics will limit their options—and that *that* is unethical. If individuals want to try an unproved treatment and if they are aware of the risks, the principle of self-determination suggests that they should be able to try even a harmful remedy. Sick and dying people, the argument goes, have a right to any treatment they desire.

The argument on the other side is that doctors, scientists, and the government have a moral responsibility to protect people from false hopes and ineffective treatments. Some insist that desperate people cannot truly exercise informed consent because their dire situation prevents them from making rational choices.

There is no clear way to reconcile the values at issue in these difficult cases, which include the patient's right to choose, the patient's right to individualized care, and society's interest in ensuring the integrity of medical science. One thing is clear, however: for many desperately ill people, experimental treatments are their only hope. For them, the outcome of the ethical debates over research on human subjects is a matter of life and death. As one such person wrote shortly after the 2000 restrictions on gene therapy experiments:

> As a person with Becker's muscular dystrophy, I am depending on successful gene therapy for my survival. . . . Scientists who study gene therapy approaches to muscular dystrophy have made substantial progress in the past few years.

> The Food and Drug Administration has acted too harshly in shutting down all gene therapy programs at the University of Pennsylvania. While the death of a patient should be taken seriously, it is no reason to shut down trials that are unrelated to that trial. Because of the FDA's action, a muscular dystrophy trial is being delayed. In addition, trials involving cancer, AIDS, cystic fibrosis and heart therapy have been shut down or delayed.

> Two children with Duchenne's muscular dystrophy (the worst type) die every day. I urge Congress to take appropriate action to make sure these trials begin again as soon as possible. They are our only hope.[14]

2

Genetic Engineering

THE DEBATE OVER whether experimental gene therapy is too dangerous to be ethically applied to humans is only one among many knotty ethical controversies that surround genetic engineering. Genetic engineering refers to the alteration of genetic material—DNA, genes, and chromosomes—to change human traits, such as susceptibility to certain diseases and disorders. Gene therapy is one type of genetic engineering.

Human DNA, the raw material of life, is composed of billions of chemical molecules, called bases, linked together in particular sequences. DNA, in turn, makes up the bodies in the cell nucleus called chromosomes, and chromosomes are divided into separately functioning segments known as genes. The nucleii of trillions of cells in a person's body contain identical copies of that person's unique DNA, including anywhere from forty thousand to one hundred thousand genes. Genes contain chemical operating instructions for human functions and traits.

A normal human being has forty-six chromosomes, arranged in twenty-three pairs. One set of twenty-three is inherited from each of a person's parents. That means that every person has two of every particular gene, or two genes relating to every function or trait. If one gene in the pair is dominant, and the other is recessive, then the dominant gene will control the function or trait in question. Often, however, neither gene is dominant, and both influence the way the body works. Also, many human characteristics are affected by more than one pair of genes.

Everybody carries some genes that are defective or that have mutations when compared to the genes' normal condition. In some cases, those genetic mutations cause diseases or make a person more susceptible to getting a disease. A major purpose of genetic engineering is to correct or override the disease-causing instructions issued by those defective genes.

But genetic engineering also creates other possibilities that many find frightening. These possibilities include the ability to bring about changes in traits that are not necessarily related

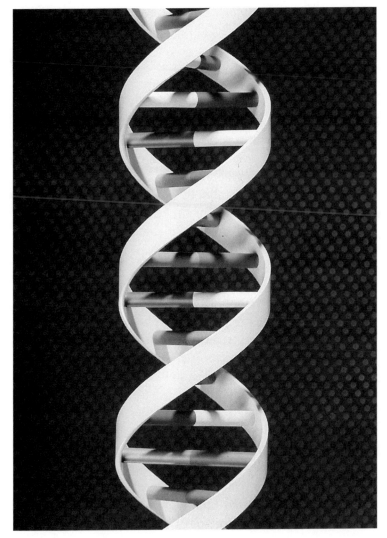

A model of human DNA, the raw material of life, which is composed of billions of interlinked chemical molecules.

to disease or disorder but make a person unique—for example, traits relating to personality, intelligence, and looks. Encoded in a person's genes are not only instructions relating to, say, how the body digests food or what triggers the growth of a tumor but also instructions relating to the brain chemistry that can cause depression and the chemistry for baldness, acne, and every other trait imaginable.

What one person may view as a condition or trait that he or she has the right to shape through genetic intervention—such as body shape or the sex of a baby—another person may believe is something that must be off limits to tinkering, for the good of society or other reasons. Genetic engineering thus presents sharp conflicts in ethical values.

Disease-fighting genes

Although, as underscored by the Jesse Gelsinger tragedy, gene therapy has yielded few clear-cut successes after hundreds of human experiments since 1990, it does seem destined to help patients with a wide variety of inheritable diseases. Among the more common of these are congenital heart defects, certain kinds of colon cancer, kidney disease, diabetes, hemophilia, Down syndrome, fragile X syndrome, sickle-cell anemia, cystic fibrosis, and Duchenne's muscular dystrophy.

Ashanthi ("Ashi") DeSilva is considered the first recipient of successful gene therapy. She was born in 1986 with a rare inherited disorder called adenosine deaminase (ADA) deficiency. ADA is an enzyme, a protein in a cell that enables a chemical reaction to take place. Because of this disorder, certain disease-fighting white blood cells in her immune system failed to produce ADA, which is necessary for their survival. As these disease-fighting cells—called T cells—died, Ashi's immune system stopped working. Ashi became extremely vulnerable to disease and infection.

When she was two years old, Ashi started taking PEG-ADA, a drug that contains the missing enzyme, ADA. Because ADA works only for a few days in the bloodstream, people with ADA deficiency need weekly shots of PEG-ADA. Although this treatment helps many children, Ashi got worse.

Because conventional treatment was not working, Ashi started receiving experimental genetic therapy treatments

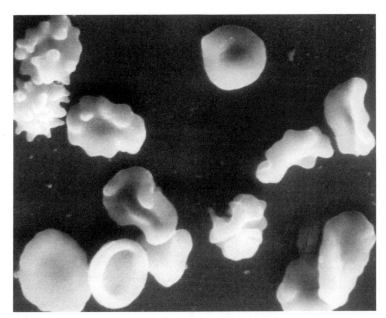

Deformed blood cells from a sample of blood taken from a person with sickle-cell anemia, a disease that gene therapy might help patients overcome.

from doctors at the National Institutes of Health in 1990. The treatments involved the removal of some of Ashi's T cells. Scientists genetically altered those cells by infecting them with a virus that was genetically engineered to carry normal ADA genes. The idea was that the T cells would end up with normal ADA genes instead of Ashi's own defective ADA genes. The cells were then injected back into Ashi's veins. Doctors repeated this process more than ten times over a two-year period until Ashi's ADA enzyme level reached 25 percent of a normal level—enough to protect her from the germs of everyday life.

Today, Ashi's genetically engineered T cells are surviving and producing ADA. As a precaution, she also continues to receive weekly PEG-ADA. Ashi cannot be said to be "cured" of her ADA deficiency, because the treatment did not spur the T cells produced by her own bone marrow to develop normal ADA genes. Still, the gene therapy made the difference between Ashi's life and death.

The "Yuk" factor

Even medical success stories, however, raise qualms about ethics. Donald Kohn, a physician who gave gene therapy to a baby boy born in 1993 with the same potentially fatal ADA deficiency that Ashi DeSilva had, felt comfortable with this form of genetic engineering, but he could understand those who do not. He explained,

> There was really a lot of resistance initially to trying this. It was seen as not just a new therapy, but a radically new paradigm [model]—putting genes into patients. We all have an internal worry about tampering with the genes. It's something primordial; it's like Frankenstein's monster. It really seems like we're tampering with the basic elements of nature.[15]

The tools for "tampering with the basic elements of nature" are now more accessible than ever before. In 2000, scientists put the concluding touches on the Human Genome Project. The outcome of that project is a map of the 3 billion chemical components, called bases, of human DNA. While the human genome map does not describe the functions of every gene, it is a key to further develop-

Human genome maps provide researchers with a blueprint of where different genes are located on human chromosomes.

ments in genetic engineering, because it provides a blueprint of where different genes are located on human chromosomes.

The disease-fighting possibilities of genetic engineering seem so great that some sardonically dismiss fears of the new technology as "the Yuk factor." Writer Oliver Morton explains: "The Yuk factor governs the initial public response to almost every biomedical advance that can easily be understood as being unnatural."[16] Deliberately infecting Ashi DeSilva, for example, with a virus to carry beneficial genes into her cells was considered "unnatural," according to Morton. But transplanting organs from dead people into sick people who need them was once viewed as "Yuk" and unacceptable, too. Indeed, Morton notes, in Great Britain, eye cornea transplants used to be illegal, even though they could save a patient's sight. In time, Morton believes, people will accept and appreciate genetic engineering, just as they do organ transplantation. "It's unnatural; it's Yuk," he writes, "but it is not bad."[17]

Journalist Walter Isaacson is also optimistic about the morality of genetic therapy and engineering. The familiar Golden Rule provides sufficient ethical guidance, he wrote in 1999:

> Do unto others as you would have them do unto you; treat each person as an individual rather than as a means to some end.

> Under this moral precept we should . . . draw a line, however fuzzy, that would permit using genetic engineering to cure disease and disabilities (cystic fibrosis, muscular dystrophy) but not to change the personal attributes that make someone an individual (IQ, physical appearance, gender and sexuality).[18]

Disease or difference

But is the Golden Rule really a sufficient answer to fears about genetic engineering? In its simplest application, it would seem a workable guide. After all, the principle of "do no harm," a close cousin of the Golden Rule, would seem to raise no ethical objections to altering human genes to prevent or treat disease.

However, a clear line does not always mark the boundary between disease and health. In some cases, what one person considers a "disease" another views as a "difference." Not even the most enthusiastic proponents of genetic engineering would argue that science should eliminate all differences in human health. The question is, Which conditions are appropriate targets of elimination through genetic technology, and which ought to be left alone—even though they are, by medical measures, abnormal?

Down syndrome, for example, is a genetic disorder that produces mild to moderate mental retardation, short stature, a somewhat flattened face, and other problems. These traits are caused by the presence of an extra chromosome in the DNA of the person who has the condition. Dr. Gregor Wolbring, an activist in the disability community, suggests that Down syndrome, while a disorder, does not rise to the level of a disease that should be targeted for "eugenic elimination":

> Down Syndrome is not a terminal disorder. It usually does not require costly medical treatment. Most reasons that lead to a eugenic decision are not in fact medical reasons, but instead are societal, educational, perceptual, and conceptual reasons. In many countries, including Western countries, Down Syndrome is considered to be a burden to society and to the family.[19]

In contrast, the always fatal Tay-Sachs disease may be viewed differently, Wolbring says, because "most people will not want to condemn a human being to a slow, early, and painful death."[20]

Although the certainty of death may be one hallmark of a disease that might be appropriately targeted for cure through genetic engineering, even this factor does not mark a clear boundary. After all, death is certain for everyone. Many people with Down syndrome, for example, die early. How early in life must a genetic disease bring about death for science to use the tools of genetic engineering against it? Must the death be painful? Aren't there disorders that may not cause their victims' deaths for many years but are still appropriate targets for genetic medicine? Alzheimer's disease, for example, strikes later in life, but many would welcome its prevention through genetic engineering.

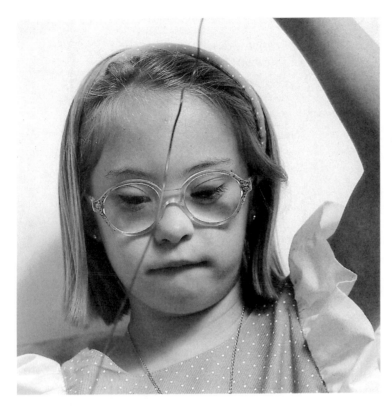

This child has Down syndrome, a genetic disorder that produces mild to moderate mental retardation, short stature, a somewhat flattened face, and other problems.

For now, there are more questions than answers about the line between disease and health—and especially about the line between disorders that are appropriate to fix through genetic engineering and conditions that should be left alone. As society works its way through the issues, perhaps the best approach is that suggested by LeRoy Walters of Georgetown University's Kennedy Institute of Ethics:

> We can applaud the war on disease that genetic research is waging. It will be a great day when a child is definitively cured of cystic fibrosis or when a particular family line is liberated from the burden of fragile X syndrome. But we will be humane warriors only if, in the midst of the battle, we also show respect for those who courageously cope with disability and for those who cannot yet be cured.[21]

Building a better human being

Through genetic engineering, scientists are capable of not only fighting disease but also changing—"improving"—

human nature. The same technologies that alter genetic material to fight disease also allow the manipulation of perfectly healthy genetic material to affect looks, athletic ability, and even intelligence. As a **PBS** program put it in 1997:

> Theoretically, all children could have the strength of an Arnold Schwarzenegger, the brilliance of Einstein, the hyperfrenetic wit of Robin Williams, and the longevity of Methuselah, all packaged together into one exquisitely fine-tuned human body.[22]

Scientists have not yet managed to create the superkid envisioned in the **PBS** program, but reality is gaining on that theoretical ideal. At the University of Pittsburgh, for example, researcher Christopher Evans is working on gene therapy for muscular dystrophy and other muscle diseases. A sports medicine doctor who heard about the treatment requested access to it to help healthy athletes develop larger muscles. In a similar vein, medical researcher Scott McIvor at the University of Minnesota was asked by a patient who wanted to change his racial appearance to be treated with genes that affect skin pigmentation.

Such requests, which probably could be fulfilled by using existing genetic engineering technology (although the side effects are unknown), make many people uncomfortable. (Both researchers above turned down the requests they received.) Altering the genetic makeup of human beings to achieve certain desired traits, whether strength, skin color, height, sociability, or hair color, smacks of eugenics—and that is a concept that carries plenty of controversial baggage.

The word *eugenics* comes from the Greek word for "wellborn." In general, eugenics refers to the improvement of the human race by selective breeding; in the context of genetic engineering, it includes the application of genetic engineering technologies to achieve this goal. The ancient Greek philosopher Plato proposed that "if we are to keep our flock at the highest pitch of excellence, there should be as many unions of the best of both sexes, and as few of the inferior, as possible. . . ."[23] The idea that people with the "best" inheritable traits should marry and have children only with one another in order to create a superior race attracted adherents even before scientists understood how traits are passed down from one generation to the next.

Of course, it is far from clear what the "best" or "superior" human traits are. Perhaps inevitably, the notion of eugenics has nearly always been used by people who claim to be superior as a basis for discriminating against those they view as inferior. In the 1920s, the American Eugenics Society successfully urged the U.S. Congress to impose restrictions on immigration of people they viewed as genetically inferior: Asians, Jews, and Slavic nationalities. Around the same time, many states adopted laws requiring the sterilization of the retarded or "feebleminded" so that their "bad genes" would not be passed down to further generations. Not coincidentally, thousands of those subjected to forced sterilization were poor or African-American. (Today, those laws no longer exist.) Also, of course, starting in the 1930s, the leaders of Nazi Germany, having decided that the German people

Hitler, seen here saluting his troops, had millions of Jews, gypsies, homosexuals, and others killed during his campaign to establish an "Aryan" race.

were in danger of being diluted by inferior genetic material, embarked on a campaign to create an "Aryan" master race, which led to the mass murder of millions of Jews, gypsies, homosexuals, and others.

High-tech eugenics

Given the sorry history of eugenics, it is not surprising that many view gene enhancements—which might be considered high-tech eugenics—with suspicion. The policy adopted by the Council on Ethical and Judicial Affairs of the American Medical Association (AMA) exemplifies this approach:

> Efforts to enhance "desirable" characteristics through the insertion of a modified or additional gene, or efforts to "improve" complex human traits—the eugenic development of offspring—are contrary not only to the ethical tradition of medicine, but also to the egalitarian values of our society. Because of the potential for abuse, genetic manipulation to affect non-disease traits may never be acceptable and perhaps should never be pursued.[24]

Critics of genetic enhancement do not argue that the technology will lead immediately to the eugenic policies of Nazi Germany. They are concerned about the many steps before that awful possibility. As one observer wondered:

> Would cosmetic gene therapy exacerbate racial or other prejudices, for example, by creating a market in preferred physical traits? Might it lead to a society of DNA haves and have-nots, and the creation of a new underclass of people unable to keep up with the genetically fortified Joneses?[25]

Despite these concerns, public opinion polls suggest that the demand for genetic enhancements may be substantial. Recent surveys indicate that as many as 45 percent of Americans approve the use of genetic engineering to improve both physical and mental traits. Even the AMA, which frowns on genetic enhancements, concedes the possibility that the technology may be unstoppable. The same policy statement that decries genetic enhancements as unethical recognizes that they may well become part of medical practice anyway. In that event, the AMA says, the ethical focus should be on ensuring that enhancements are not made at the price of harmful side effects.

Proponents of genetic enhancement state that it is not much different from cosmetic surgery, which society has accepted for decades.

Proponents of genetic enhancement defend its morality on several grounds. First, they point out that genetic engineering is a voluntary individual treatment, far different from state-imposed eugenic policies, such as those enforced by Nazi Germany. Second, they say that genetic engineering to produce cosmetic changes is not that different from cosmetic surgery, which society has accepted for decades. Third, society encourages measures such as improved diets and exercise to promote everything from increased height to stronger muscles to clearer minds—and genetic engineering is merely another tool to achieve these aims.

Supporters of genetic enhancement also argue that because the line between cosmetic enhancements and medical treatment is often

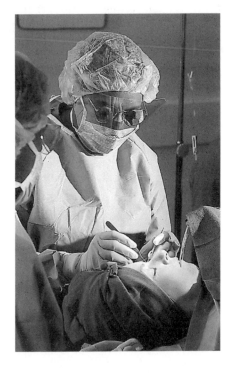

fuzzy, barring enhancements while permitting medical therapy would be arbitrary and unfair. Short stature, for example, is not necessarily a medical problem, yet today doctors sometimes treat it with a synthetic version of the human growth hormone that spurs greater height. Once scientists refine genetic engineering techniques so that they can alter the genetic material that triggers growth, should they be forbidden from treating a child with that gene therapy on the grounds that an unusually short child is not a sick child? If that is the case, some argue, then doses of growth hormone must also be suspect.

Avoiding "defective" offspring

One way to engineer a person's genetic makeup is to do it before that person is even born. In theory, scientists could tinker with the DNA of human egg and sperm cells to determine at least some of the traits that the resulting children will receive. This is called germline engineering, and some critics find it extremely suspect on ethical grounds. The primary argument against germline engineering is that the current generation does not have the right to make decisions that will so fundamentally alter future generations. Others argue, however, that germline engineering is no more suspect than any other type of genetic manipulation and that it should be available to families who want to rid themselves of terrible hereditary diseases, such as sickle-cell anemia and hemophilia, that otherwise will shadow generation after generation.

For now, germline engineering is more of a future possibility than a current reality. Another type of genetic engineering, however, is currently available for creating babies that have certain genetic traits. This method, called genetic selection or preimplantation genetic diagnosis, can be used when a mother undergoes in vitro fertilization, or IVF. IVF has been used for years to help couples who have difficulty conceiving children. In IVF, some of a woman's eggs are removed from her ovaries and incubated in a laboratory with sperm. After some of the eggs are fertilized by the sperm, they divide and grow into tiny embryos. These embryos—usually more than one, because of the risk of failure—are then implanted into the mother's womb, where, if things go well, at least one continues growing into a fetus and baby.

Today, scientists are able to screen the laboratory embryos very early in their development—when they are no more than eight cells large—for certain genetic characteristics. Embryos that carry harmful genetic mutations can be discarded, and only embryos exhibiting no known genetic defects can be implanted into the mother's uterus.

In recent years, this type of genetic selection of babies conceived in vitro has been used by parents whose genes carry a high risk of passing on serious inheritable diseases, such as Tay-Sachs disease and Huntington's disease. Dr. Angela Christiano, an expert in a genetic disease called epidermolysis bullosa, which causes babies to be born without skin and sometimes without coverings for their internal organs, enrolled couples who had already had one child with the excruciating disease in a program of preimplantation

A nurse inspects the quality and health of sperm that are going to be used for in vitro fertilization.

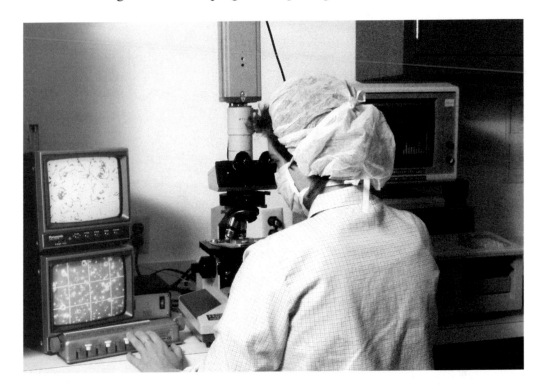

genetic diagnosis. "To actually know that we have the potential to determine whether that embryo would live and develop into a healthy human being, or die from a lethal, terrible, painful disease in six months to me was an awesome moment,"[26] Christiano said.

Some oppose preimplantation genetic diagnosis on the grounds that the discarded genetically defective embryos are human life, which should not be destroyed. They see no difference between early genetic intervention resulting in discarded embryos and abortion, which they also oppose. Others raise concerns that the ability of some parents to select against "defective" babies while others continue to give birth without first testing and selecting their embryonic offspring will make society less tolerant of people with disabilities. According to writer Catherine Baker:

> We also need to worry about whether genetic technology will make us less accepting of people who are different. For example, if it is possible to predict and prevent the birth of a child with a gene-related disorder, how will we react to children we meet who have that disorder? Will we think, Why is this child alive? Will we think, Why didn't the parents "do something" to prevent the child's condition? Will we resent the medical and special education costs spent on the child? Will we put pressure on parents not to have "defective" children?[27]

The AMA's stance is that ethical considerations require a balancing approach to the issue. The AMA's current ethical policy explains:

> In general, it is ethically permissible for physicians to participate in genetic selection to prevent genetic disease. However, selection to avoid a genetic disease may not always be appropriate, depending on factors such as the severity of the disease, the probability of its occurrence, the age at onset, and the time of gestation at which selection would occur. It would not be ethical to engage in selection on the basis of non-disease related characteristics or traits.[28]

Designer babies

The last sentence in the AMA policy statement—"It would not be ethical to engage in selection on the basis of non-disease related characteristics or traits"—points to the

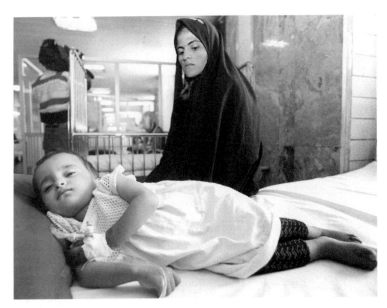

Gender identification and selection has been used to help parents avoid giving birth to children with diseases such as hydrocephalus, the condition from which this child suffers.

most controversial current issue in genetic selection: choosing a baby's sex. Gender identification and selection were first used to help parents avoid giving birth to infants with catastrophic diseases, such as certain types of hydrocephalus (water on the brain), hemophilia, and Duchenne's muscular dystrophy. These conditions, as well as such others as fragile X syndrome, are linked to the so-called X chromosome and appear only in boys. By examining the genetic material of early embryos created through in vitro fertilization, doctors can identify those destined to grow into boys and avoid them when selecting embryos for implantation.

What started out as a medical tool, however, now does double duty as a lifestyle device. More and more patients at in vitro fertilization clinics are using preimplantation genetic diagnosis to select the desired gender of their offspring for non-disease–related reasons. Gender selection has attracted vocal critics, many of whom are generally more concerned about what the practice might lead to than what it actually represents. "Sex selection is a precedent for Eugenics with a big E, not the little E," says University of Virginia bioethicist John Fletcher. "If you want to go down this road of getting the human genetics movements off track, this is the first stop."[29]

The fear of those opposed to genetically engineered gender selection in embryos is that once society puts a stamp of approval on selecting "desirable" traits—beginning with gender—discrimination and inequities will surely follow. In 1997, one British doctor opened an IVF clinic with gender selection to attract patients from cultures that place a great emphasis on the ability of a mother to produce a male heir. The reaction of American physician Angela Christiano was this: "I think it's an outrage. I can't believe someone is abusing the technology in this way. It's fundamentally a sexist decision."[30]

Others see gender selection differently and recall that other reproductive technologies were also viewed with horror when first introduced but then became commonplace. Another argument made in favor of the ethics of gender selection technology is that there is no meaningful distinction between using genetic engineering to prevent the birth of babies with inheritable diseases—a use that many people applaud—and employing the same technology to select desired traits (gender and otherwise) in embryos. As writer Robert Wright argues:

> But what is the difference? Therapists consider learning disabilities to be medical problems, and if we find a way to diagnose and remedy them before birth, we'll be raising scores on IQ tests. Should we tell parents they can't do that, that the state has decided they must have a child with dyslexia [a learning disability]? Minor memory flaws? Below average verbal skills? At some point you cross the line between handicap and inconvenience, but people will disagree about where.[31]

Where society draws the line—between handicap and inconvenience, disease and difference, medical intervention and cosmetic enhancement—and what rules apply on the two sides of the line are critical issues. They determine how far science can go in trying to change humanity's inborn characteristics. They determine how far particular individuals can go in trying to change the hand they were dealt at birth. It is no exaggeration to say that the decisions that society makes regarding the ethics of genetic engineering will determine the future of humanity.

3

The Promise and Perils of Information

WHILE MUCH OF the promise of the revolution in genetic knowledge lies in the future—when scientists hope to produce dramatic cures through genetic engineering—one thing the revolution has already produced in abundance is information. These days, scientists uncover a new human gene nearly every week. They have developed blood tests that can tell people whether they are carriers of disease-related genetic mutations. Among these are tests that detect the genetic mutations associated with Alzheimer's disease, some types of breast and ovarian cancer, cystic fibrosis, Duchenne's muscular dystrophy, fragile X syndrome, Huntington's disease, sickle-cell anemia, and some forms of hemophilia. In 1999, U.S. laboratories performed 4 million genetic tests.

These new tests for prying personal medical information out of an individual's genes are only the latest additions to an already well stocked toolbox of devices that gather personal health data. Such devices include blood tests for communicable viruses, such as HIV (which causes AIDS), charts and records relating to doctor and hospital visits, and prescription drug records from pharmacies. Much of the information gathered through these tools is stored in computers, included in databases, and available online. The United States today is experiencing a medical information explosion as the amounts and types of medical information and the means to store and share it expand daily.

Personal medical information is a powerful resource. Test results, for example, may help individuals better understand their susceptibility to cancer and cause them to adopt lifestyle changes that reduce the risk of actually contracting that disease. Individual health data can also be useful to the health of society as a whole. If public officials know the incidence of communicable diseases, such as AIDS or tuberculosis, among individuals in a community, they can take steps to prevent the spread of those illnesses to others.

Personal medical information is powerful, but it can also be harmful to an individual's reputation and livelihood. If members of a community learn, for example, that their family doctor has tested positive for HIV, they may find another doctor. If an employer finds out that a key employee has prescriptions for multiple psychiatric medicines, the employer may conclude that the employee is too unstable to do his or her job. Medical information, then, is a double-edged sword, capable of both benefiting and harming the individuals that it concerns.

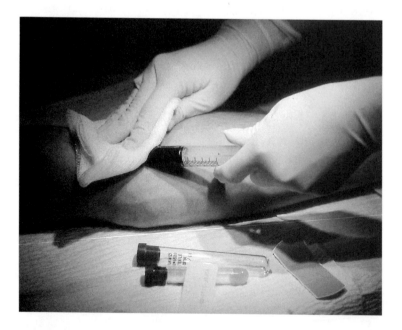

Blood tests are one means that doctors use to gather information about their patients' health.

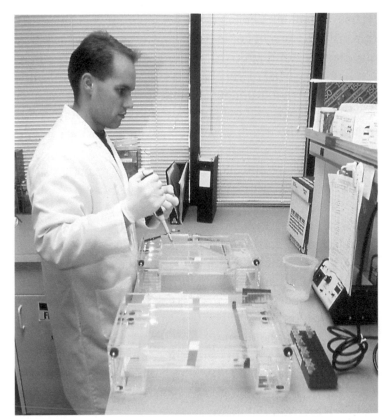

Though the practice is controversial, there is little doubt that genetic testing can be beneficial and lifesaving.

Genetic tests

There is little question that genetic testing can be beneficial and even lifesaving. Ann Miscoi, for example, used to feel sick all the time. She was always tired, she told *Newsweek* magazine, her joints hurt, and her hair was falling out. At first, her doctor told her nothing was seriously wrong. But Miscoi knew that her father and her uncle had died of multiple organ failures in their forties, and she was concerned that she might have inherited a genetic disorder. She found a new doctor who knew about a recently developed genetic test for a condition known as hemochromatosis, in which the body stores harmful amounts of iron in organs, tissues, and blood.

Symptoms for hemochromatosis usually appear in mid-life (Miscoi was 50), and include organ damage, diabetes, and heart problems. Doctors know how to treat hemochro-matosis—the problem has always been how to detect it.

Before researchers isolated the hemochromatosis gene defect in 1996, many people died unnecessarily because their disease was not diagnosed and left untreated. Today, people like Ann Miscoi can have a simple blood test to uncover the hemochromatosis gene and get the treatment they require. Miscoi now has regular treatments for her hemochromatosis, which was detected and controlled before it caused any lasting harm.

Even when the information revealed by genetic testing is less conclusive, it can be useful. A gene test may show, for example, that a person carries a mutation that is sometimes associated with a disease, such as cancer. That does not necessarily mean the person is definitely going to get cancer. What it means is that the person has a higher risk of getting cancer than a person who does not have the genetic mutation. A person who tests positive for familial adenomatous polyposis, an inherited type of colon cancer, can have his or her doctor adopt a more aggressive program of monitoring and removing growths in the colon. This practice has improved the health of many who might otherwise have let these growths go undetected, become cancerous, and perhaps even kill them.

Information gap

In many cases, however, scientists have not yet figured out what to do with the information that genetic tests provide. Although researchers have made great progress in identifying genetic mutations through screening tests, the progress in developing treatments for diseases associated with genetic mutations has been much slower. This gap between the ability to extract genetic data and the capacity to treat genetic disorders can be problematic.

For example, Huntington's disease is a terrible neurological condition that affects one in ten thousand people. It is caused by a mutation in a single, dominant gene. The disease generally strikes in middle age as the mutation produces a gradual failure in the parts of the brain that control movement. A person who suffers from Huntington's disease experiences mild symptoms first, such as mood changes.

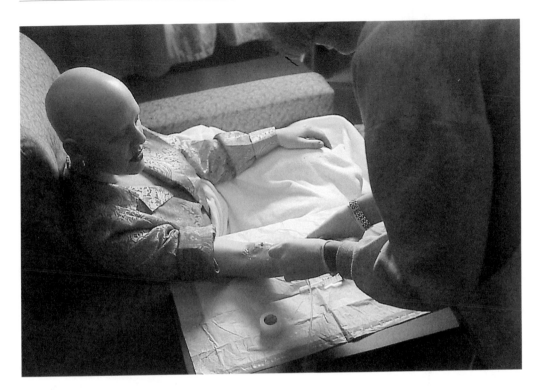

Then other symptoms develop, including twitching of the arms and legs. These worsen until the person is unable to talk, to control his or her movements, to walk, and to eat. Huntington's disease always kills its victims, and there is no known cure. Scientists have developed a screening test for the genetic mutation for Huntington's disease, however. This leads to the question, If a person's parent had the disease, should that person be tested to see whether he or she inherited it?

A person who is currently healthy but who is found to carry the genetic defect for Huntington's knows only that he or she will get the disease. When the disease will strike, and what its course will be—a gradual decline or a swift one—these questions are not answered by the genetic screening test. At the same time, many difficult questions are raised by a finding of the genetic mutation for Huntington's disease. Should the carrier tell a serious boyfriend or girlfriend before marriage is proposed? After all, there is a 100 percent chance that the carrier will die

Gene tests can be helpful in determining whether a person carries the mutation that is sometimes associated with cancer.

from the disease. What should be done about having children? Should an employer be informed? Because the knowledge that someone is a carrier of the Huntington's disease mutation puts the patient in a difficult position with respect to others and because the knowledge is of no use in treating the patient, some believe that genetic screening for this disease is inappropriate.

The principle of individual autonomy, however, seems to favor testing even for incurable genetic disorders, such as Huntington's disease. Armed with the knowledge that one's life will end prematurely, a person might take action to enrich the years that he or she does have. This is arguably an important and ethical function of medical information: to take realistic stock of one's health and life expectancy and to plan accordingly.

Steven Peterson is an example of a person who wanted to know whether he had inherited the genetic mutation for a rare and debilitating neurological disease. His grandmother suffered from spinocerebellar ataxia, which gradually causes its victims to lose all muscle control, and his father was diagnosed at age forty-five. There is no cure for spinocerebellar ataxia, but there is a genetic test. Peterson took it when he was in his mid-thirties and found out that he does, in fact, carry the defective gene. His reaction was to make financial arrangements for his wife and three children, solidify his family business— and buy a new Harley Davidson motorcycle. "Knowing I have this [genetic disorder] has enabled me to take control of my life,"[32] he told a magazine reporter in April 2000.

Ambiguous results

Most disease-related genetic mutations are not dominant, as the Huntington's disease defect is, which means that their presence is not a sure sign of future illness. A positive result (meaning that the mutation being tested for was found) on a genetic screening test indicates that an individual has a higher risk than normal for the disease associated with the mutation—but not that the individual will definitely get the disease. This ambiguity raises practical and ethical issues with respect to the use of genetic tests.

The most heated ethical debate concerns relatively new tests marketed by commercial laboratories to the public for various types of cancer and Alzheimer's disease. The labs target their services to people who have a strong family history of the disorder in question. A negative result—meaning that the individual does not carry the defective gene—is good news. But even a normal test result does not necessarily mean that the individual will not later get, for example, cancer. Tests do not detect every genetic mutation that might cause cancer, and cancer often strikes regardless of "good" genetic test results. One danger of genetic tests, then, is that normal results might give people a false sense of security and might encourage them to be less vigilant in monitoring their health or pursuing a healthful lifestyle than they otherwise would.

A positive result on a genetic test—meaning that the defective gene associated with a particular disease is present—is also problematic. For example, a positive result from a currently available test for different mutations of the gene associated with Alzheimer's disease does not mean that the tested individual will definitely contract the disease. Nor does it indicate how severe a case of Alzheimer's the person will get (if he or she gets it) or when the disease will develop. Yet a person who tests positive on an Alzheimer's gene test may experience serious psychological and social problems. If the information is shared with an employer, the person may suffer adverse consequences at work, too. Accordingly, many genetics experts and ethicists believe that the benefit to be gained from the ambiguous information extracted by the Alzheimer's gene test is dwarfed by the harmful effects that can occur, and they discourage use of the test.

Because of difficulties in interpreting many gene tests, genetic counseling has emerged as a new field in the medical arena. Genetic counselors help people understand the

Genetic counselors help people understand the results of genetic tests.

results of their tests, including the ambiguities. Assistance provided by genetic counselors can help remedy some of the confusion that genetic testing may produce, which, in turn, reduces the ethical dilemmas. Even with genetic counseling, however, ethical questions about genetic testing remain unresolved.

Public health, private problems

The ethical problems of what to do with personal medical information did not originate with the recent advent of genetic testing. These problems have been arising since the early days of American history. At least one American colony, Rhode Island, had a law as early as the 1740s requiring tavern keepers to tell local officials whether any of their customers appeared to have contagious diseases. By 1900, every state had enacted laws requiring reports to local officials of communicable diseases, such as smallpox, cholera, and tuberculosis.

These laws and their modern counterparts reflect an important function of government: protecting the public health.

One way government officials carry out this function is through the collection and analysis of information about the medical condition of millions of individuals. A central purpose of this information gathering has been, and continues to be, identifying people who have communicable and fatal diseases, such as tuberculosis, typhoid, smallpox, and, today, AIDS. In the past, public health officials often imposed quarantines, or required periods of isolation, on people who carried such diseases as a way to control their spread. Today, officials are more likely to educate people about how communicable illnesses are transmitted and how to reduce the risks of transmission.

When public officials have access to information about individual cases of communicable diseases, they can also develop strategies to eradicate those diseases. The battle against the deadly smallpox virus, for example, was won in large part because local public health officials were able to identify outbreaks of the disease promptly and vaccinate individuals who were at risk of contracting it. More recently,

Public health officials believe that the best way to control the spread of AIDS and other communicable diseases is through education.

when doctors reported unexplained deaths among otherwise healthy individuals in the southwestern United States to public health officials, the information helped scientists quickly identify and prevent the transmission of a new type of hanta virus—undoubtedly saving lives.

Important as the goals of public health laws and policies are, they can be at odds with individual privacy interests. The right of a person to keep information about his or her health a secret and to require his or her doctor to respect this secrecy has been acknowledged for thousands of years. Part of the Hippocratic oath (the pledge sworn to by new physicians, which is believed to date from approximately the fifth century B.C.) reads: "Whatsoever things I see or hear concerning the life of men, in my attendance on the sick or even apart therefrom, which ought not be noised abroad, I will keep silence thereon, counting such things to be as sacred secrets."[33]

Several reasons and concerns support the principle that a doctor or other health care provider should keep a patient's health information confidential. People often see or speak with their doctors, sharing intimate details of their lives, when they are physically and mentally vulnerable. To take information that is gathered in such a setting of dependency and trust and turn it over to strangers (namely, government officials) strikes many as unfair behavior and a breach of trust. In addition, the principle of individual autonomy supports the notion that an individual has the right to control his or her health information, including the right to prevent doctors from disclosing it to others.

Another argument in favor of maintaining a wall of privacy around personal medical information is that confidentiality is a central component of any relationship between doctor and patient. Indeed, it is the very expectation of privacy that encourages patients to be honest about their health when talking to doctors. If this expectation were diminished, some observers fear, people would be more guarded in their conversations with doctors. This could lead to health care decisions based on incomplete or poor information or a failure to obtain needed treatment because

Patients are more likely to give honest accounts of their medical conditions to their doctors if they trust that the information will be kept confidential.

patients keep information from their doctors. In fact, a January 1999 survey found that one in six U.S. adults had concealed facts about their health, sometimes from their doctors.

The AIDS challenge

The conflict between an individual's right to shield private medical information from public view and the public interest in protecting and enhancing the health of all members of society is sharply presented in society's response to the AIDS epidemic. Doctors now know that AIDS is caused by the human immunodeficiency virus, or HIV. A simple blood test, available since 1985, can tell a person if he or she has HIV and is therefore at risk of developing AIDS. Valuable as the information gathered from this test can be, both to the individual tested and to public health officials, it is also dangerous. As a 1997 report by legal and ethics experts explained, "Testing for HIV . . . is unlike most other tests performed in the medical setting. The psychological and social impacts of a positive result, including the increased risk of possible suicide, are important to consider."[34]

Despite the dangers, the principle of individual autonomy has been forced to bend in the face of AIDS. Many states have laws that require doctors or health officials to notify spouses or sexual partners that they may have been exposed to HIV on the basis of an individual's test results. Some jurisdictions require health officials to trace other persons who may have been exposed. State law may also permit disclosure of HIV test results to enable health officials to study the spread of the virus.

States have enacted laws that prevent the results of HIV tests, such as the ones being conducted here, from being disseminated too broadly.

Along with laws requiring the disclosure to government officials of information about individuals who are HIV positive, states also have enacted laws preventing government officials and others from disseminating this information too broadly. The protections afforded vary greatly from state to state. Such laws, as well as the general pro-

fessionalism exhibited by those who work in the health care system, do help keep private information out of the public eye. Professor Lawrence Gostin and other scholars in a 1997 study concluded:

> For their part, health departments have a generally excellent history of maintaining the confidentiality of personal information. Disclosure to health departments (as opposed to family, friends, employers, or insurers) seldom produces tangible harm such as stigmatization, embarrassment, loss of employment, or denial of insurance.[35]

Nonetheless, many people are concerned about the confidentiality of personal health data collected by government agencies and have called for stronger legislation to ensure the protection of individual privacy.

Data deluge

Government agencies are not the only organizations whose activities raise privacy concerns about the collection and dissemination of personal medical information. Doctors and other health care providers, as well as employers and insurance companies, also gather medical data that individuals might prefer to keep private. However, while the government's data activities generally focus on public health goals, these other collectors of medical information are usually motivated by a very different objective: ensuring the smooth and profitable operation of the complicated health care and health insurance system.

Health insurance is a contract that many Americans buy from private insurance companies, receive as a benefit from their employers, or obtain from the government. Under a health insurance policy, or contract, the insurer promises to pay for certain health care services that an individual (the insured person) may need. The insured person pays a set amount, called a premium, to the insurer in advance. (Alternatively, the payment can be made by an individual's employer if the insurance policy is a work benefit.) In any given year, some people will receive medical services worth more than the amount of their premium, and others will pay premiums that exceed their medical expenses. An insurance company can both pay for its customers' medical needs and make a profit if the amount it has to pay out for medical care is less than the amount of money it takes in.

There are many types of health insurance, as well as businesses—health maintenance organizations, or HMOs, are the best known—that have developed in an effort to provide health care at lower costs. What they all have in common is the need for personal medical information. They need individuals who apply for insurance to give them accurate information about medical conditions so that premiums can be set appropriately. They need doctors who treat insured individuals to give them information on patients' conditions and treatments so that payments for medical services can be calculated properly. They need pharmacists who dispense medicines, which insurers may also pay for, to provide details about what medicines insured patients receive. Often, personal medical information is entered into computer databases, where it can be easily accessed by those who need it.

Many Americans are concerned about the degree to which the health care system is dependent on the collection and sharing of personal medical information. There is some evidence to support their fears about losing control of their own personal health data. In 1997, Donna Shalala, the U.S. secretary of Health and Human Services, gave a congressional committee examples of a health data system out of control:

> Until recently, at a Boston-based HMO, every single clinical employee could tap into patients' computer records and see detailed notes from psycho-therapy sessions. In Colorado, a medical student copied countless health records at night and sold them to medical malpractice attorneys looking to win easy cases. And, in a major American city, a local newspaper published information about a congressional candidate's attempted suicide. Information she thought was safe and private at a local hospital. She was wrong.[36]

Like state health officials, doctors, health insurers, and others are also limited to some extent by laws that shield personal health data. A majority of states require physicians and hospitals to keep patient records confidential, permitting disclosure only with the written consent of the patient. But patients frequently sign consent forms when they see a doctor or visit a hospital, authorizing the health care provider to release medical records to insurers, and sometimes employers, so that payment will be made. In the eyes of critics, this is the weak link in the chain that protects patient confidentiality.

Many states do not have laws that specifically require insurers or employers to respect the privacy of personal medical information. The gaps and inconsistencies in state-by-state legal protections for personal medical data have prompted calls for uniform federal rules. However, deciding what the best course is for protecting personal medical data has proved to be a difficult and controversial task. People disagree on such issues as whether some categories of health data should be granted less protection than others for public health or policy considerations. Given the growing uses of personal health information and the massive volume of data, the debate over the best way to protect

Health insurance providers need pharmacists to provide details about what medicines their clients receive.

individual privacy in a complex health care system is not likely to conclude anytime soon.

Data-based discrimination

Among the reasons a person might want to shield his or her personal medical information from disclosure, the fear of discrimination is central. A little data can go a long way in harming a person. Employers who learn about employees' visits to doctors and therapists, or the results of predictive genetic tests, or the outcomes of diagnostic blood tests might use that information to limit job opportunities. The problem is not limited to the workplace. Discrimination based on information about an individual's medical condition occurs in such settings as doctors' offices and schools as well. Many are also concerned about the use of medical data by health insurance companies to exclude a person from obtaining insurance because, for example, that person has tested positive for a genetic mutation that increases his or her risk of cancer.

The rise of AIDS and HIV testing pushed the discrimination issue to the forefront in the past decade. People who have been diagnosed with AIDS or found to be HIV positive

Demonstrators march in an effort to promote AIDS research and awareness. Some people with AIDS have lost their jobs or been excluded from schools because of the disease.

have encountered, and continue to encounter, prejudice and discrimination. They have lost their jobs and been excluded from schools. In response, lawmakers have enacted measures designed to decrease discrimination against people who have tested positive for HIV or who have AIDS. Some state laws prohibit such discrimination. On the national level, the 1990 federal Americans with Disabilities Act (ADA) outlaws discrimination against people with disabilities, including people who are HIV positive or have AIDS. The law covers discrimination in employment, public accommodations, such as restaurants, medical offices, and other settings.

No law, however, necessarily changes the way people think. For example, HIV and AIDS continue to mark its victims with a stigma because of the virus's association with sexual activity and drug use. Despite the protections guaranteed by the ADA, therefore, many people with HIV infection, AIDS, and other disorders are still at risk if information about their medical status is disclosed.

Genetic injustice

If AIDS marked the beginning of an era of heightened awareness of unfair treatment based on the results of medical testing (the blood test for HIV), the recent advent of genetic tests has emerged as a new flash point in the debate over unethical and discriminatory uses of personal medical data. A 1998 federal government report disclosed numerous instances of workplace discrimination based on genetic information. One man who applied for a job told the employer that he carried a mutation for Gaucher disease, an inheritable enzyme deficiency. As the carrier of this mutation, he was at risk of passing the disorder on to his children but would not necessarily develop symptoms himself. Nonetheless, the employer refused to hire him on the basis of his genes. Another man interviewing for a job revealed that he had hemochromatosis but did not have symptoms of the disease. At his second interview with the company, a company representative told him that the company was interested in hiring him but could not offer him health insurance (a common employee benefit) because of his genetic condition. Although he agreed to this limitation, at his third interview, the company representative told him that he would not be hired after all because of his genetic condition.

This outbreak of genetic data-based discrimination has not gone unnoticed by lawmakers and policymakers. More than two-thirds of the states have laws limiting discrimination in health insurance based on genetic tests; some states also bar genetic-based employment discrimination. A federal law, the 1996 Health Insurance Portability and Accountability Act, also provides a limited amount of protection from discrimination by insurance companies. In the workplace, the federal ADA covers discrimination against people who have symptoms as a result of a genetic disorder—they are considered "disabled" under the law—but its application to individuals who carry genetic mutations but are otherwise healthy is less clear.

Of course, insurers, employers, and similar organizations do have tangible interests in genetic test results. The healthier the pool of people covered by insurance, the less money the insurer has to pay out to doctors and patients, and the more money it can keep as profit. The knowledge that a woman is genetically at a higher risk than normal of contracting breast or ovarian cancer can therefore be useful to an insurer looking for ways to identify and turn away risky candidates, thus keeping down costs. Some insurers worry that when people discover that they carry a potentially harmful genetic mutation, they will buy insurance, incur high medical costs, and drive up the cost of insurance for everyone. That is why, these companies argue, they are entitled to have access to genetic test results. Similarly, some employers are concerned about hiring people who have hidden genetic defects that will later prove to be detrimental.

Francis Collins, who heads up the National Human Genome Research Institute, has said, "Everyone is a mutant."[37] His point is that everyone has genetic mutations. Some are useful, some are harmful, and many are still a mystery. As the explosion in genetic information about these countless mutations continues to erupt, the American legal, health care, and business systems will need to come to terms with the promises and perils presented by the explosion. The goal of any ethical resolution in this area is to balance the concerns of individuals in maintaining their privacy against the legitimate interests of others who may be affected by an individual's medical condition. The hard part, however, is not to balance anyone's legitimate interests out of existence.

4

Organ Transplants

ON MARCH 14, 2000, National Basketball Association star Sean Elliott took to the floor of the Alamodome, the home court of his team, the San Antonio Spurs, and played basketball. As he headed for a dunk, Elliott slipped and fell to the floor. He quickly got up. Later in the quarter, he drove to the basket again, only to be stopped by opponent Dikembe Mutombo of the Atlanta Hawks, who sent Elliott down again, this time on his back. The hometown crowd was not amused.

Basketball is a physical sport, with its share of pratfalls and elbow jabs. Elliott's falls were not unusual, and Mutombo hadn't been playing unfairly. Spurs fans were aware, however, that the game marked Sean Elliott's first time on the court since receiving an organ transplant seven months earlier. The starting forward had been suffering from advanced kidney disease. Sean Elliott's older brother Noel had donated one of his own kidneys for the transplant, which was performed in August 1999. By March 2000, Noel was back to his usual life of working for a Tucson aerospace company. And Sean was back to his usual life as an NBA star. The fans at the Alamodome did not have to worry. After his encounter with Dikembe Mutombo, Sean Elliott picked himself up and kept on playing.

Organ transplants save many lives every year. Doctors are able to replace about twenty-five different organs and tissues in the human body—including kidneys, livers, lungs, hearts, and intestines—with substitutes from other humans. Some recipients of donated organs are well known, like Sean Elliott, who was the first athlete in a major professional sport to return to his game after a transplant. Some, like Elliott, receive their organs from a relative or other living donors. Most transplant patients, however, receive organs from people who have recently died—generally healthy people killed by accidents.

What all organ transplant recipients share in common is that they are winners in the race against their illnesses—whether kidney disease, cirrhosis of the liver, heart disease, or others—which would kill them if they did not receive new organs. Unfortunately, organ transplant patients compete against other desperately sick people as well. Far fewer organs are available for transplantation than there are patients who need them. Some seventy thousand people in the United States need organ

Basketball player Sean Elliott (left) received a kidney donation from his older brother, Noel (right).

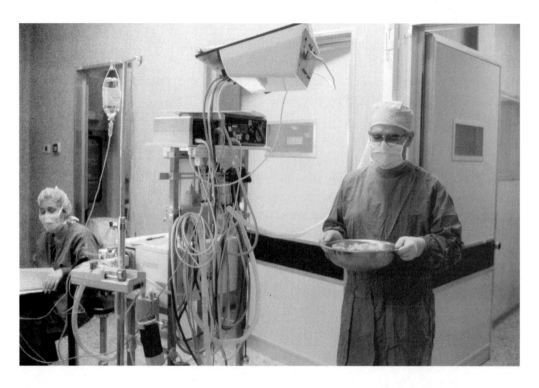

The shortage of cadaver organs raises ethical concerns about how to allocate them.

transplants. In 1999, however, fewer than twenty-two thousand transplants were performed because of the shortage of organs. That year, six thousand people died awaiting transplants.

The shortage of cadaver organs—that is, organs from the bodies of people who have recently died—creates ethical dilemmas that are both poignant and practical. Organs must be allocated in some fashion among the patients who need them, but because organs are in short supply, any system of allocation leads to winners and losers. Even careful efforts to allocate scarce organs and to boost the number of people who can receive transplants will lead to fairness concerns. When people are competing for life itself—which is what is at stake in organ transplantation—the rules of competition and the way life-and-death decisions are made become acutely important.

Waiting lists

The United Network for Organ Sharing (UNOS) is in charge of allocating cadaver organs for transplant in the

United States. UNOS is a private organization that operates the allocation system under an agreement with the U.S. Department of Health and Human Services. The organization maintains a national waiting list of patients who need transplants. It also has a computer network linking hospitals that perform transplants and those that harvest, or retrieve, organs suitable for transplantation.

UNOS allocates organs according to a formula that takes into account a number of factors. These include how sick a patient is, how long he or she has been on the UNOS waiting list, how far the patient is from the organ donor, and the size of the organ. Additional rules apply, depending on the type of organ in question. UNOS also supervises how doctors and hospitals harvest organs.

In practice, the organ transplant system involves a series of complex evaluations. In the case of a person with liver disease, for example, the person must first be found to have end-stage liver failure. But doctors at the transplant hospital where the patient applies for evaluation must also determine that he or she is healthy enough to survive and adapt to the transplant, so that a patient must be seriously ill but not too seriously ill. In addition, the transplant team of doctors, nurses, and social workers must find that the patient has enough money (or insurance), family support, competency, and personal stability to manage the complicated care that follows transplant surgery.

If a patient passes these qualifying tests, then he or she is put on the UNOS waiting list. Where a person stands in the line when an organ becomes available depends not only on the length of time he or she has been on the list but also on his or her condition (the sickest get top priority) and on geography.

But the system is made still more complex by the demands of medical science. A person who needs an organ cannot use just anyone's organ. The donor and the recipient must have compatible blood and tissue types. If the donor and the recipient do not match, the recipient's body will reject the organ. So even if a person makes it to the top of the waiting list, he or she may have to pass on an available organ because it is not compatible.

Scientific considerations are also behind some of the other UNOS allocation rules. A cadaver organ must be transplanted quickly, before it deteriorates. This time constraint supports the geographic rules that favor distributing some organs to recipients who are closest to the donors.

The result of the application of these rules and considerations can be a new lease on life for those lucky enough to reach the top of the waiting list. Leah Horchler, for example, was born with liver disease. She grew up in Phoenix, Arizona, where, because of her illness, she was unable to ride a bicycle, play sports, or do other physical activities. Other children posed a threat to her, because if she caught a cold or other common infection from them, she might become very sick. When Leah was nine years old, doctors determined that her liver had deteriorated so much that she needed a new one. She was put on the waiting list.

About a year later, in December 1994, Leah's family received a fateful call: there was a liver for her. She underwent surgery that same day. Less than two weeks later, Leah was able to go home from the hospital; less than a month after her surgery, Leah went ice-skating for the first time. Although Leah will have to take medicine for the rest of her life to help prevent her body's immune system from rejecting her transplanted liver, she is not complaining. "The best part about life since my transplant is that I'm not in the hospital so much," Leah told the magazine *Contact Kids*. "I'm healthy and normal."[38] After her surgery, Leah learned that her liver had come from a six-year-old girl who had died in an automobile accident.

Rewriting the list

For every Leah Horchler who receives a life-giving organ transplant, there are many more patients who wait and die while waiting. Some critics blame the organ allocation system, arguing that it suffers from practical and ethical flaws. Among the most controversial features of the system have been its geographical preferences. Announcing a plan to change organ transplant policies, U.S. Secretary of Health and Human Services Donna Shalala said in 1998,

U.S. Secretary of Health and Human Services Donna Shalala believed that organs should go to the sickest patients first.

My concern is that people are dying unnecessarily, not because they don't have health insurance, not because they don't have access to care, but simply because of where they live in this country. There is no medical reason to restrict these organs within arbitrary boundaries.[39]

Critics such as Shalala believe that organs should go to the sickest patients first, without regard to where those patients live. Such a change, they argue, would spread the supply of scarce organs over a larger population, reducing the great disparities in waiting times that otherwise exist in different regions around the country.

Responding to such criticism, in the spring of 2000, UNOS agreed to change its allocation rules to broaden the geographic distribution of organs and to move more organs to the sickest patients. Livers, for example, now would be shipped farther to reach patients in worse condition than those living closer to the donors. The method of evaluating potential organ recipients would be weighted more heavily in favor of patients with the most urgent need.

Still, the organ allocation system is constantly changing. Some state officials and their allies in the U.S. Congress are opposed to efforts to centralize decision making about transplants. Political leaders in Wisconsin, for example, have expressed fear of a loss of control over transplant policy in their state, where organ donation rates are high in comparison to the rest of the country. Patients in Wisconsin have generally received organs faster than in other states. But under a national distribution system, many of its livers could be directed to Chicago, with a large population of would-be transplant patients. Opponents of a national system of organ allocation also fear that it would lead to unnecessary deaths by giving organs to patients who are too sick to benefit from them and depriving healthier patients of a chance at survival.

No system of allocating transplant organs can satisfy all critics or serve all values. The principle of equal treatment for all patients will sometimes conflict with the principle that organs should go to patients who have the money and support to take care of themselves and their new organs after surgery. The neutral principle of first-come, first-served will sometimes conflict with the principle that a person in immediate, dire circumstances should not die simply because he or she didn't get in line quickly enough. These conflicts between worthwhile values—and the ethical dilemmas of organ transplant policy—seem destined to persist for as long as patients need organ transplants to survive and organs remain in short supply.

Undeserving patients?

While even opponents in the organ allocation debate agree that equal treatment of similarly situated patients is an important goal of transplant policy, others argue that not all patients are similarly situated. This argument arises particularly in the context of liver transplants. Many patients who need new livers were born with diseased livers, developed liver disease through no fault of their own, or suffered traumatic damage to their livers as a result of accidents. But a significant number of people need new livers because they destroyed their own by excessive drinking of alcohol. Whether these patients should be granted access to an extremely scarce resource on the same terms as other patients has been a hotly debated question.

The main argument for bypassing alcoholic patients is that they are said to bear a moral responsibility for their condition and therefore should not be permitted to take away a needed organ from a blameless patient. This is why some people were uncomfortable when baseball legend Mickey Mantle and Woodstock-era musician David Crosby obtained liver transplants. Such critics acknowledge that alcoholism is a disease and not merely a bad habit or moral weakness. But, they say, alcoholism is a treatable disease. People with the disease must take responsibility for it and obtain treatment, much the same way people with chronic diabetes must watch their diets and administer insulin shots to themselves.

Traditionally, doctors and other health care practitioners have accepted an ethical responsibility to treat all people

Some people thought Mickey Mantle (pictured) was undeserving of the liver transplant he received because his health problems were caused in part by his own alcohol abuse.

who need medical care, regardless of the cause of that need. Many physicians and ethicists still adhere to this principle and reject the notion that alcoholics should be treated less favorably than other patients vying for liver transplants. One such group, writing in the *Journal of the American Medical Association,* argues:

> Moral evaluation is wisely and rightly excluded from all deliberations of who should be treated and how. . . . We do not seek to determine whether a particular transplant candidate is an abusive parent or a dutiful daughter, whether candidates cheat on their income taxes or their spouses, or whether potential recipients pay their parking tickets or routinely lie when they think it is in their best interests.[40]

Such inquiries into a patient's moral virtue not only would be intrusive, the argument continues, but also would lead to arbitrary results. Doctors and other decision makers, scattered in hospitals across the country, cannot reach consistent judgments about what behaviors

" A man found your wallet with your organ donor card. He doesn't want a reward but he will accept a kidney."

are so blameworthy as to disqualify a patient from treatment.

In a society that is based in large part in the principles of equality and self-determination, the debate over transplants for patients with alcohol-damaged livers touches a sensitive nerve. The value of equality suggests that all patients in need should be treated the same, regardless of what caused their disease. The value of self-determination points in the opposite direction: If people make their own choices freely, then they should live with the consequences of those personal choices. So far, U.S. policy has mostly reflected the principle of equality. If liver shortages persist or grow worse in the future, the pressure to shift to a policy reflecting a different principle may prove irresistible.

Increasing the supply

An obvious way to reduce waiting lists for organ transplants is to increase the number of people whose organs are donated when they die. One reason for the organ shortage in the United States is that many Americans seem ambivalent about whether they want organs harvested from their bodies, even though they know their organs can mean the difference between life and death for another person. For example, in a Gallup poll, only 37 percent of Americans said they were "very likely" to want their organs transplanted after their death, and only 32 percent "somewhat likely."[41] Also, 55 percent said they were willing to grant formal permission for their organs to be donated upon their death, yet only 28 percent had actually done so.

The Uniform Anatomical Gift Act provides the legal framework for organ donations. In effect in all the states and Washington, D.C., the law recognizes the legal status of donor cards signed by people to express their desire to be organ donors in the event of their death. For people who do not fill out the cards, the law gives a deceased person's family the authority to make an organ donation if the person did not express opposition to donation.

Advocates for increased organ donations view this system of voluntary donation as flawed and ineffective. Few people sign and carry their donor cards, often not because they oppose donation, but rather because the subject of death and organ harvesting is unpleasant to contemplate. Also, even when a person has signed a donor card, hospital officials may still ask the family for consent upon his or her death. Although this reflects sensitivity to the individual's grieving survivors, it seems to contradict the rule in the Uniform Anatomical Gift Act that an intended donor's wishes be followed. In addition, it undermines the autonomy of the deceased, particularly the right to decide the issue for himself or herself.

In a situation where an individual has not signed a donor card, doctors and nurses attending to his or her death may fail to ask the family about the possibility of organ donation. Again, this lapse reflects concern for the surviving family's emotional condition. The deaths of potential donors are usually sudden and traumatic, and hospital personnel wish to avoid further upsetting the families. Some doctors and ethicists also believe that family members facing the unexpected death of a loved one—who is often a young person—cannot be counted on to think clearly in such a charged emotional state and therefore are not capable of giving truly informed and voluntary consent. This reasoning suggests that obtaining permission for organ harvesting in these circumstances is not ethical.

The perceived practical and ethical problems with the organ procurement system in the United States has given rise to a number of proposals for change. Some advocate new legislation that would require doctors or other medical personnel to ask family members about organ donation in the absence of a donor card. Others suggest a system of "mandated choice," in which all adults would be required by law to decide whether they wished to donate organs upon their deaths. An individual could easily change his or her decision, but in the event of death, the family could not override it. Some favor enacting a law that allows a person to be an organ recipient only if he or she earlier agreed to be an organ donor.

Rules and proposals about when the organs of a person may be donated upon his or her death implicate the basic relationship of an individual to society. Some may believe that society's need for more organs for transplantation justifies measures that may override an individual's or a family's in-

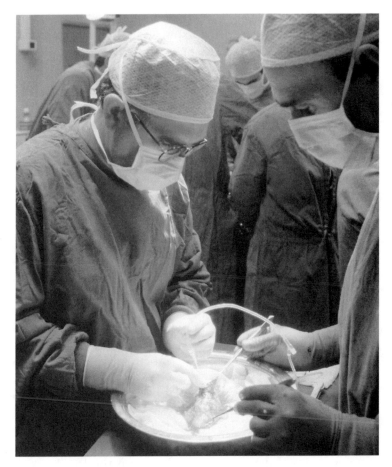

Complicated ethical questions about organ procurement have arisen due to society's need for more organs for transplantation.

decision (or even opposition) to organ harvesting. Others believe that individual choice is the more important ethical value and that any system of rules for organ donation must honor that above all. Clearly the right to decide what to do with one's own body is a fundamental American precept. The challenge posed in the organ donation context is that, very often, people never get around to exercising that right before they die—and then the choice must be exercised by others.

Living donors

In light of the severe shortage of cadaver organs, in recent years, doctors and patients have looked to living donors for organ transplants. A healthy person needs only one kidney and might donate his or her second kidney to a person in need. A person might also donate half of his or her liver to a liver-diseased person, and both the donor and the recipient will recover, each partial liver regenerating into a whole healthy liver within a matter of weeks. Live donation is also possible for lungs, pancreases, and intestines. Transplants from living donors have other benefits for the organ recipients. For example, operations can be scheduled in advance, instead of being performed on an emergency basis, as is the case with cadaver organs. Also, live donor transplants eliminate the need to go through painstaking efforts to preserve, store, and ship organs.

While the great majority of all organ transplants come from cadavers, living donors are on the rise. According to the United Network for Organ Sharing, living liver donation increased by more than 200 percent from 1998 to 1999, and more than one-third of transplanted kidneys in 1998 came from living donors. In most cases, the donors are family members. But transplants from friends, co-workers, religious congregants—even strangers—have become more common.

In April 1999, Ken Schuler, of Linville, Virginia, underwent ten hours of surgery so that doctors could give half of his liver to a woman who had been a stranger to him until twenty days earlier. He heard of Deborah Parker's desperate search for a matching liver donor on the local news. Parker's liver had failed as a result of hepatitis she had contracted from a blood transfusion during gallbladder surgery fifteen years earlier. Schuler contacted her and, once he was found to be a match, went forward with the transplant, which transplant experts believe to be the first from a living donor with no previous relationship with the recipient. Schuler explained: "If I was standing on a riverbank and saw somebody drowning, I wouldn't care whether it was a stranger or somebody I knew. I couldn't stand there and watch him drown." He also told a reporter: "It makes me feel better than anything I've ever done in my life."[42]

Living donor transplants raise a set of ethical questions separate from the dilemmas posed by cadaver transplants.

Such donations seem to breach the primary rule of the doctor's Hippocratic oath: "First, do no harm." A living donor undergoes major surgery, risking harmful bleeding, infection, and complications from anesthesia. The risk of dying is estimated at about three out of ten thousand surgeries. Although nearly all living donors appear to come through the transplant experience with no problems, some doctors and ethicists are concerned that when a healthy person is subjected to permanent injury and risk for the sake of another, an ethical line is crossed. Jeffrey P. Kahn, director of the Center for Biomedical Ethics at the University of Minnesota, explains:

> Deliberately maiming, or even killing one patient to help or save another cannot be construed as a morally acceptable medical decision, no matter how willing the patients. Trading the health or welfare of one person for another runs counter to our basic societal beliefs about justice and the rights of individuals—for instance, we don't allow slavery, even by willing parties.[43]

Many ethicists, including Kahn, are willing for doctors to participate in some types of living donor transplants, particularly if the risk to the donor is low and the donor's motives are acceptable to society, such as a parent donating an organ to his or her child. The issue becomes more muddled, however, when the donor and the recipient are unrelated or when they do not even know each other. The main concern of doctors and ethicists in these cases is that the donor's decision is truly informed, rational, and unselfish. Cheryl Jacobs, a clinical social worker with the transplant team at the University of Minnesota hospital, says:

> Whether it's religion or wanting to turn over a new leaf—whatever the motivation is, we need to know it. But we don't have a cookbook text to tell us about what's allowable and what's not—other than if the donor is getting paid, which is clearly forbidden.[44]

Parts for sale

If living donors are willing to give their organs to one another in exchange for the satisfaction of doing a good deed, it seems reasonable to assume that even more people would donate their organs in exchange for something more tangible—namely, money. Nevertheless, although ten patients die daily in the United States for want of an organ transplant, U.S. law forbids the sale of human organs.

This prohibition stems from English common law, the unwritten law based on tradition and court decisions, but it has modern justifications as well. Opponents of commerce in human organs cite philosophical problems in treating the body as property. They argue that a market for organs would transform people into products, cheapen respect for life, and undermine the notion that humans are intrinsically worthwhile. Poor people especially would be pressured into selling their own organs (as living donors) and those of their deceased relatives. More practically, critics worry that if organs could be bought and sold, voluntary organ donations would fall off, resulting in fewer organs available for transplant overall.

Those who favor organ sales acknowledge that poor people would be swayed to sell their organs, but they argue that doing this would benefit the sellers. Money earned from organ sales could then be used for their own medical expenses or funeral costs. Proponents also point out that money is exchanged at every step of the transplant process—hospitals, doctors, the people who work at transplant procurement organizations all get paid—and that donors are the only ones left out.

Despite the desperate need for an increased supply of transplant organs, revulsion at sales of human organs in the United States runs deep. The status quo, in which financial compensation is banned, is unlikely to change anytime soon, and patients in need of new organs will continue to compete with one another for a chance at life.

5

Assisted Suicide

WHILE MANY PATIENTS wage difficult and poignant battles to overcome disease and hang on to their lives, others seek a different form of relief: death. Their struggles can be every bit as difficult and touching as those of patients fighting for life. People with terminal diseases (that is, diseases for which there is no cure and that lead to death), conditions that cause terrible physical pain, or illnesses that are severely debilitating, sometimes want to end their lives. This desire becomes a matter of medical ethics when a patient seeks a doctor's assistance in dying.

Doctors and others in the medical field normally work to save lives, not to end them. As the AMA's Council on Ethical and Judicial Affairs has stated, "Physician-assisted suicide is fundamentally incompatible with the physician's role as healer. . . ."[45] The AMA's view, which is also the view of many lawmakers and citizens, is that "allowing physicians to participate in assisted suicide would cause more harm than good."[46] This conclusion is reflected in the laws of nearly all the states, which prohibit doctors from assisting in a patient's suicide, whether by prescribing a lethal dose of drugs or other means.

On the other hand, as long ago as ancient Greece, philosophers such as Plato and Aristotle favored *euthanasia,* or "easy death." Modern medical technology has forced society today to face the conflict between the doctor's role as healer and the principle that human beings should not be forced to suffer through a horrible death. As

Barbara Coombs Lee of the group Compassion in Dying testified before a panel of the U.S. House of Representatives:

> The problem is that medical science has conquered the gentle and peaceful deaths and left the humiliating and agonizing to run their relentless downhill course. The suffering of these individuals is not trivial and it is not addressed by anything medical science has to offer. Faced with this dilemma, the problem for many is that the law turns loving families into criminals. It encourages patients to choose violent and premature deaths while they still have the strength to act. And it forces some to suffer through a slow and agonizing death that contradicts the very meaning and fabric of their lives.[47]

The Greek philosopher Plato was an advocate of euthanasia, or "easy death."

Defining the debate

The debate on assisted suicide is often hampered by confusion over the meaning of related but conceptually distinct terms. According to the AMA, physician-assisted suicide occurs,

> when a physician facilitates a patient's death by providing the necessary means and/or information to enable the patient to perform the life-ending act (e.g., the physician provides sleeping pills and information about the lethal dose, while aware that the patient may commit suicide).[48]

A different situation is presented when a doctor withholds or withdraws treatment at a patient's request and that patient dies. For example, very ill patients may be kept alive through the use of respirators (which mechanically enable them to continue breathing), renal dialysis (which cleanses the blood of toxins, or poisons), and feeding tubes. When life-sustaining treatment is withheld, the patient dies mainly because of an underlying illness that, left untreated, overcomes the patient's weakened defenses. As Felicia Cohn of the Institute of Medicine in Washington, D.C., explains:

> [T]here's a big difference between letting someone go and assisting their suicide, and legally there's a difference. . . . [A] right to physician assisted suicide does not necessarily logically follow from a right to forego life sustaining treatment. All of us right now can choose to forego any medical treatment that we don't wish to have or don't wish to impose on the loved ones for whom we are making decisions. We don't all have the right to assist those loved ones in suicide. . . .[49]

A patient's right to the termination of life-sustaining treatment is often referred to as the right to die. If a patient is unconscious or otherwise unable to express his or her wishes (because of mental illness or other conditions that leave a person incompetent), a family member or close friend may seek the cessation of treatment on the patient's behalf. This is also generally considered an assertion of the patient's right to die.

Some ethicists and legal scholars say that the claim by others of an incompetent person's right to die is a poten-

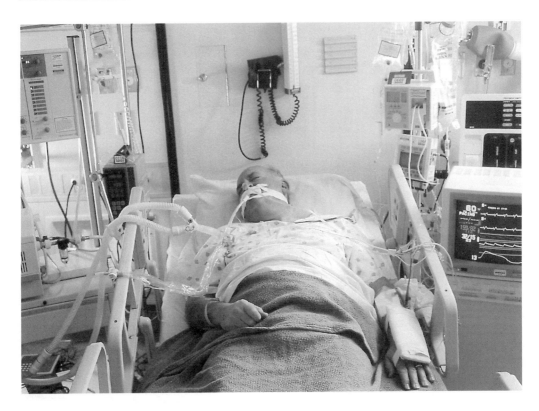

tially dangerous practice. Whenever society allows people to claim a right to die on behalf of others, they say, society edges closer to acceptance of euthanasia, also known as mercy killing. By euthanasia or mercy killing, these critics mean a practice of putting to death people who, in the judgment of others, are better off dead. That judgment may be well intended, as in the case of a nurse or doctor who knows an unconscious patient is suffering horribly. The real fear, of course, is that those with decision-making power will decide to euthanize others whom they view as undesirable or burdensome.

Some people claim that society comes closer to an acceptance of euthanasia when it allows family members or close friends of a terminally ill patient to decide whether to let the patient die.

Legal aspects

In recent years, judges and legislators have addressed legal issues relating to the withdrawal of medical treatment (and the related right to die) and physician-assisted suicide. In a 1990 case, the U.S. Supreme Court faced the question of whether a person has a right to die by refusing

unwanted medical treatment. In that case, a young Missouri woman named Nancy Beth Cruzan fell into a state of indefinite unconsciousness after a car wreck. Because she was unconscious, Nancy was unable to eat or swallow on her own, so doctors inserted a feeding tube in her stomach to give her nutrition and medication. With the tube, Nancy could be kept alive indefinitely; without it, she would die. After watching their daughter remain in this state of permanent unconsciousness for more than four years with no real hope of recovery, Nancy's parents sought a court ruling so that doctors would have to remove the feeding tube. They argued that Nancy herself would have chosen to die under the circumstances and that she had a right to die that the courts should enforce.

The case made its way through the judicial system and ended up in the U.S. Supreme Court. Opponents of Nancy's parents argued that no one, not even parents, should be able to decide to bring about another person's death. They likened Nancy to a disabled person, such as a child with autism or an aged person with a degenerative disease. To remove such a person's feeding tube, they argued, was no different from starving that person to death. Allowing Nancy's parents to direct doctors to take steps that would lead to Nancy's death was not an exercise of a "right to die," they insisted. It was the first step on a slippery slope to euthanasia of people whom society considers undesirable.

The Supreme Court's decision gave something to both sides of the issue. An individual does have a constitutional right to refuse lifesaving treatment, the Court said, including food and water. This right derives from the notion that a part of the liberty guaranteed by the U.S. Constitution is the right to be free from unwanted touching and to protect the integrity of one's own body. But when a case involves a person who has become unconscious without expressing his or her wishes on the matter, a state may require clear and convincing evidence of that person's desire to discontinue life support before allowing doctors or family to terminate such treatment.

A few months after this ruling, Nancy's parents went back to court in Missouri armed with new evidence of their daughter's preference to die rather than remain in a persistent vegetative state. The evidence included statements from three of Nancy's friends who remembered conversations in which Nancy said she would never want to live hooked up to a machine. Nancy's doctor, who had previously opposed removing the feeding tube, also testified for Nancy's parents, describing in graphic detail Nancy's life: stomach problems, eye problems, bleeding gums, obesity, contorted limbs, seizures, and vomiting, all while she lay unconscious. This time the courts gave Nancy Cruzan's parents the permission they sought and her feeding tube was removed on December 15, 1990. She died twelve days later after being unconscious for eight years.

Right to die, not license to kill

In 1997, the Supreme Court addressed the question of physician-assisted suicide when challenges were brought to

New York and Washington state laws that banned the practice. In this case, the Court found no support in the Constitution for a right to assisted suicide. States were free to ban assisted suicide, the Court held, to further society's interest in protecting vulnerable individuals and to reinforce the American tradition of valuing human life. "The state's assisted suicide ban reflects and reinforces its policy that the lives of the terminally ill, disabled, and elderly people must be no less valued than the lives of the young and healthy," Chief Justice William H. Rehnquist wrote. He also drew a distinction between death from the withdrawal of life support, which was at issue in the earlier case of Nancy Cruzan, and assisted suicide: "[W]hen a patient refuses life-sustaining medical treatment, he dies from an underlying

Chief Justice William H. Rehnquist, writer of the Supreme Court's 1997 ruling against physician-assisted suicide.

fatal disease or pathology," the chief justice wrote, "but if a patient ingests lethal medication prescribed by a physician, he is killed by that medication."[50]

Opponents of assisted suicide praised the decision. New York attorney general Dennis C. Vacco said, "This ruling will protect Americans from a regime that says it's cheaper to kill patients than to treat them."[51] Some proponents of assisted suicide were defiant. One Washington, D.C., physician who treated many patients with AIDS—and who helped several terminally ill patients die by prescribing lethal overdoses of medicine—told a newspaper reporter, "I don't care what the court says. If that is what my patient wants and what the family wants and what I want, we are going to do it."[52] Other proponents noted that while the Supreme Court decision said the U.S. Constitution does not provide a right to assisted suicide, it left open the possibility for states to legalize the practice if they choose. Officials of such organizations as the Hemlock Society and Compassion in Dying vowed to continuing working for state legislation of that kind.

So far, Oregon is the only state to enact a law that permits physician-assisted suicide. The Oregon Death with Dignity Act took effect in late 1997. Under the act, a physician may give a mentally competent adult who is suffering from a terminal illness a prescription for lethal medication. The law imposes numerous safeguards to ensure that a patient makes a decision that is both voluntary and informed. For example, the patient must make the request for assisted suicide in person and in writing. The request must be made repeatedly, with waiting periods between requests. Patients are required to obtain second opinions on their medical condition and to receive counseling on alternatives that might reduce their pain or make them more comfortable. Doctors must keep records of assisted suicide cases. The law does not allow a doctor or anyone else to end a patient's life by lethal injection.

Practicing terminal medicine

Courts and legislators may establish rules and boundaries about assisted suicide, but in practice it is doctors and other medical professionals who must respond to patients who say they want to end their lives. Many turn such requests away, often because of doubts about or opposition to assisted suicide. In fact, according to a 1999 report by the Oregon Health Department on the effects of the law during its first year, 40 percent of doctors refused to prescribe drug overdoses, mainly because of their moral qualms about the practice.

The Oregon Health Department report said that fifteen people went through with physician-assisted suicide during the first year of the Oregon law. Thirteen of them had advanced cancer. Other patients obtained their prescriptions for lethal overdoses but either died of their diseases first or simply chose to continue living. One of these was Barry Kurath, who suffered from cancer, as well as AIDS contracted from a blood transfusion. He died in July 1999 at age forty-seven, after years of illness—but of natural causes, not from the drugs he had obtained from a doctor under the Death with Dignity Act. Kurath never used them, but, according to his girlfriend, they provided him with an important sense of control over his own care and destiny.

In February 2000, the *New England Journal of Medicine* published a more detailed study covering the first two years of Oregon law. This study found that after a person made a request for assisted suicide, doctors often instituted changes in the person's health care, such as improving pain control, prescribing psychiatric medicine to help with disorders such as depression, or referring the patient to a mental health counselor or to hospice care. About 15 percent of those who requested physician-assisted suicide in Oregon changed their minds, often after doctors made these changes.

The February 2000 study also found that the primary concern of the patients who expressed an interest in assisted suicide law was the loss of independence they had experienced, or would experience, as their health declined. By the end of 1999, forty-three people had died as a result of lethal prescriptions obtained under the Oregon law, although ten times as many had taken the first step of asking a doctor for assistance in dying.

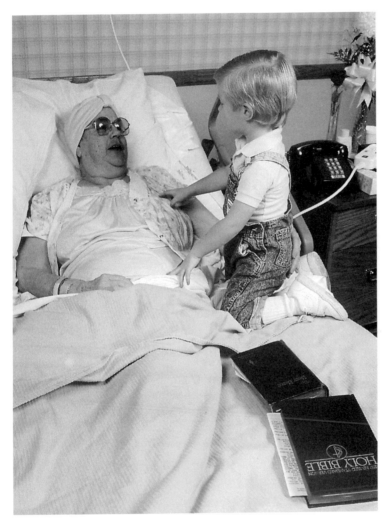

Instituting changes to a patient's health care, such as referring a patient to hospice care, may help change the minds of individuals who have requested assisted suicide.

Proponents of the Oregon law cite the 1999 and 2000 reports as evidence that the statute was working in an appropriate and ethical manner, providing relief to a small number of patients who, after deliberation and counseling, chose to die. Fears that the law would be used by people who suffered from treatable depression or pain were unfounded, its supporters say, as were concerns that the vulnerable and disadvantaged would feel pressured—by family members and by doctors—to use the law to kill themselves. Advocates also argue that the ability to obtain a legal lethal overdose serves to strengthen patients' sense

Dr. Jack Kevorkian agreed to assist patients with suicide despite the legal consequences.

of autonomy or self-determination. This may end up actually preventing some suicides, since patients feel less despair if they know they can control their final days.

Others are not so sure. They point out that several people in the Oregon studies sought to kill themselves to avoid pain and that a more appropriate response to such patients is better and more aggressive pain management. The fact that those who used the Oregon law were several times more likely to be divorced or never married than those in the general population raised the question of whether people were dying out of loneliness—and whether society might have a better response for that problem, too.

"Dr. Death" and beyond

The practice of physician-assisted suicide is not limited to Oregon. Doctors across the country receive requests for aid in dying and sometimes accede to them, even though their actions may be illegal. Dr. Jack Kevorkian, also known as "Dr. Death," is the most infamous physician who has readily concurred in requests for assisted suicide despite the legal consequences. Kevorkian has assisted in more than one hundred suicides and was acquitted several times of violating various laws against assisted suicide. In April 1999, however, Kevorkian was convicted of second-degree murder in a Michigan state court for assisting in the suicide of Thomas Youk, who had suffered from amyotrophic lateral sclerosis (ALS), a degenerative muscle disease, also known as Lou Gehrig's disease. Kevorkian gave Youk a lethal injection and then gave a videotape of the event to the television show *60 Minutes,* which broadcast it on November 22, 1998. "I only intended to do my duty," he argued during his trial. "Medical service is exempt from certain laws."[53] Kevorkian was sentenced to ten to twenty-five years in prison.

Few doctors share Kevorkian's disdain for the law, but a significant number are willing to assist in patients' suicides in some circumstances. A national survey published in the *New England Journal of Medicine* in 1998 indicates that patient requests for assisted suicide are not rare. More than 18 percent of doctors reported having received a request from a patient for assistance with suicide; 11.1 percent had been asked for a lethal injection. Of the doctors receiving such requests, 16 percent said they had written at least one prescription to be used to bring about death, and 4.7 percent said they had administered a lethal injection. Also, 11 percent of doctors said that under current law—which generally prohibits physician-assisted suicide (except in Oregon)—they would still be willing to prescribe a death-inducing prescription in some circumstances, and 7 percent said they would provide a lethal injection. If assisted suicide and euthanasia were legal, 36 and 24 percent, respectively, said they would engage in those practices in certain situations.

These studies and other evidence make plain what most doctors already know, according to Dr. Charles F. McKhann:

"Physicians have always helped some patients to die."[54] The question is whether or not this widely practiced yet unacknowledged phenomenon is ethical. McKhann, a cancer surgeon, believes there is a place in medicine and in medical ethics for a doctor to aid a suffering patient's "rational suicide." As he writes:

> A society that prohibits assisted death to a suffering person and another society that puts to death those who are burdensome have one serious defect in common. Both are placing society's interest far ahead of the freedom of the individual. In doing so, they are equally mistaken and equally dangerous.[55]

This point of view elevates the principle of individual self-determination over other competing values, most notably the sanctity of life. People who take this position generally agree that safeguards, such as mental health evaluations and counseling, are appropriate to ensure that a patient's decision truly is autonomous and not influenced by others. But if a patient of sound mind and in hopeless health clearly asks for help in dying, this argument goes, the ethical course of action is to respect that person's choice.

Compassion or abandonment?

Others believe it is immoral to help people kill themselves, even if that is what they say they want. "Killing one another is not compassionate, it's abandonment," said William Toffler when the Oregon Death with Dignity Act was being debated. "Why are we judging these lives as worthless when in fact their lives aren't worthless? They have the right to live."[56] Doctors and society in general have a duty, this argument maintains, to preserve life, not end it—even if this means overruling the express desires of a person seeking assisted suicide.

For many who oppose physician-assisted suicide on ethical grounds, an underlying premise of their argument is that a person who requests suicide is by definition not making a rational choice. The requester needs to be told of the options—medication, counseling, other forms of assistance—that make suicide an irrational choice. In addition, for those who believe

that suicide is unethical because it violates the sanctity of life, physician-assisted suicide is unethical for the same reason.

Opponents of assisted suicide also fear that it will lead inevitably to euthanasia or mercy killing of people deemed undesirable. Several advocacy groups for people with disabilities are against physician-assisted suicide for this reason. For example, the Advocacy Center for Persons with Disabilities, a Florida agency, stated in a legal brief that it filed in a Florida lawsuit relating to assisted suicide:

Advocates of physician-assisted suicide believe that society's interests do not outweigh the interests of suffering patients.

> To give someone, including a physician, the right to assist a person with a severe disability in killing himself or herself is discrimination based on a disability. It lessens the value of a person's life based on health status and subjects persons with severe physical and mental disabilities to undue pressure to which they may be especially vulnerable. . . . If assisted suicide is permitted in Florida, Floridians will be put on the so-called slippery slope of determining the relative value of life. Floridians with severe physical and mental disabilities, who are particularly vulnerable to being devalued as burdens of society, would be at grave risk.[57]

The future of death—and ethics

Controversies over end-of-life issues, such as assisted suicide, are perhaps inevitable in today's society, where the average life span is around seventy-seven, and most people die of ailments that persist for months or years before death. Americans enjoy longer lives today than in the past, but for some that means long periods of suffering.

Many ethicists and doctors, regardless of their views of the morality of assisted suicide, believe that society has an obligation to provide better alternatives. Ethicist Arthur Caplan has suggested that a starting point is to recognize that mere pain is not what drives most people to choose assisted suicide—suffering is:

> Severe disability, loss of cognitive function, loss of self-esteem, frailness, and dependency are what people have in mind to avoid if they can choose physician-assisted suicide. . . .

> The real issue for many who favor assisted suicide is that it provides a way out of a future that some do not wish to endure. If you suffer from a massive stroke, Alzheimer's disease, severe multiple sclerosis, massive burns, a paralyzing injury, ALS, or Parkinsonism, you are not terminally ill. You may not even be in pain. But you most assuredly could find yourself suffering, either anticipating or enduring those dread afflictions.

America's longer average life span means prolonged periods of suffering for some patients.

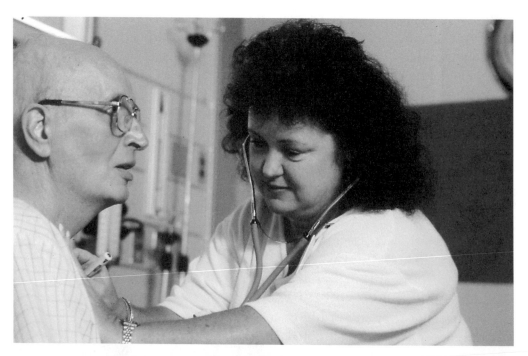

> The moral challenge medicine and nursing face is what to do about the management of suffering, not pain. Suffering is far broader than pain.[58]

This perception seems to be borne out by the February 2000 study of the Oregon Death with Dignity Act. Susan Tolle, head of the Center for Ethics in Health Care at Oregon Health Sciences University, said:

> There was a fear of future suffering, and, possibly, a lack of trust that the medical profession will be there for you at the end, that was manifest in this study. If fear of future suffering is one of the things we learn to address, then it may be that fewer people would follow through in taking a lethal prescription.[59]

Addressing the fears that lead people to seek their own death is a complicated matter. Many experts believe that treating pain, diagnosing and treating depression, and letting patients know that much pain and suffering can be greatly reduced are key elements in preventing people from choosing assisted suicide. Religious leaders say that communities need to offer families more support—moral and practical—as they go through health problems or deal with chronic or terminal illness. Some say that more education about so-called living wills and advance medical directives—in which people write down in advance if and when they want medical treatment discontinued—would relieve fears. The idea is that fewer people would seek assisted suicide as a means of avoiding future suffering if they could legally ensure that at least some forms of suffering—such as being kept alive by a respirator or feeding tube—would not be inflicted on them.

Legal scholar and philosopher Ronald Dworkin wrote, "Making someone die in a way others approve, but he believes a horrifying contradiction of this life, is a devastating, odious form of tyranny."[60] On the other hand, the danger posed by physician-assisted suicide is that it could permit some people—families of patients, doctors, even government officials—to make or unduly influence decisions that the lives of others are not worth living. This, too, would be a "devastating, odious form of tyranny."

The function of medical ethics in this area is to guide the medical profession and society to resolutions that avoid either form of tyranny. This is no easy task in an arena where contradiction between ethical values—respect for the sanctity of human life, relieving human suffering, respect for an individual's choices, protection of the weak and vulnerable—is commonplace. But conflict between competing values is the recurrent and defining theme throughout medical ethics. As medical science continues to advance and to create new choices in health care, the role of medical ethics will continue to be providing individuals, doctors, and society with the means to sort through the conflicting values and to reach decisions that reflect the best moral and practical values possible.

Notes

Introduction

1. Quoted in Alan Fleischman, "Medical Futility: How Much Is Too Much and Who Should Decide?" *Pediatric Ethicscope,* Spring & Summer 1998, p. 2.

2. Quoted in Jeffrey P. Kahn, "When the Cure Seems Worse than the Disease," *CNN Interactive,* October 6, 1998. www.cnn.com.

Chapter 1: Experimental Treatments

3. Quoted in Beverly Woodward, "Challenges to Human Subject Protections in US Medical Research," *Journal of the American Medical Association,* November 24, 1999. www.jama.com.

4. Sheila Kaplan and Shannon Brownlee, "Duke's Hazards," *U.S. News & World Report,* May 24, 1999. www.usnews.com.

5. Quoted in Sheila Kaplan and Shannon Brownlee, "Dying for a Cure," *U.S. News & World Report,* October 11, 1999. www.usnews.com.

6. Gary B. Ellis, "Protecting the Rights and Welfare of Human Research Subjects," *Academic Medicine*, September 1999. www.aamc.org.

7. Quoted in Woodward, "Challenges to Human Subject Protections."

8. Quoted in Woodward, "Challenges to Human Subject Protections."

9. Quoted in Kaplan and Brownlee, "Dying for a Cure."

10. Deborah Nelson and Rick Weiss, "Hasty Decisions in the Race to a Cure?" *Washington Post,* November 21, 1999, p. A1.

11. Quoted in Rick Weiss and Deborah Nelson, "FDA Halts Experiments on Genes at University," *Washington Post,* January 22, 2000, pp. A1, A12.

12. Quoted in Rick Weiss and Deborah Nelson, "Victim's Dad Faults Gene Therapy Team," *Washington Post,* February 3, 2000, pp. A1, A2.

13. Quoted in Rick Weiss, "Monitoring Tightened for Genetic Research," *Washington Post,* March 8, 2000, p. A3.

14. Brad Stephenson, Letter to the Editor, *Washington Post,* March 19, 2000, p. B6.

Chapter 2: Genetic Engineering

15. Quoted in "A Genetic Rescue for a Tattered Immune System?" in *PBS Online,* "Cracking the Code," aired December 16, 1997. www.pbs.org.

16. Morton, "Overcoming Yuk," *Wired,* January 1998. www.wired.com.

17. Morton, "Overcoming Yuk."

18. Walter Isaacson, "The Biotech Century," *Time,* January 11, 1999. www.time.com/time/magazine.

19. Gregor Wolbring, "Eugenics, Euthenics, Euphenics," *Gene Watch,* a bulletin of the Council for Responsible Genetics, June 1999. www.genewatch.org/genewatch/genejun.html.

20. Wolbring, "Eugenics, Euthenics, Euphenics."

21. LeRoy Walters, "Ethical Issues in Human Gene Therapy," *Human Genome News,* February 1999. www.ornl. gov/hgmis/publicat/hgn/hgn.html.

22. "Eugenics," in *PBS Online,* "Cracking the Code," aired December 16, 1997. www.pbs.org.

23. Plato, *The Republic of Plato,* Francis MacDonald Cornford, ed. and trans. New York: Oxford University Press, 1975, p. 159.

24. American Medical Association, "Current Opinions of the Council on Ethical and Judicial Affairs," E-2.11. www.ama-assn.org.

25. Rick Weiss, "Gene Enhancements' Thorny Ethical Traits," *Washington Post,* October 12, 1997, p. A1.

26. Quoted in "Sifting the Genes of Life and Death," in *PBS Online,* "Cracking the Code," aired December 16, 1997. www.pbs.org.

27. Catherine Baker, *Your Genes, Your Choices: Exploring the Issues Raised by Genetic Research,* Chapter 7, a publication

of Science + Literacy for Health, a project of the American Association for the Advancement of Science Directorate for Education and Human Resources. ehrweb.aaas.org/ehr/books/7_dr.html.

28. American Medical Association, "Current Opinions of the Council on Ethical and Judicial Affairs." E-2.12. www.ama-assn.org

29. Quoted in "The High Technology Way to Select a Baby's Sex," in *PBS Online,* "Cracking the Code," aired December 16, 1997. www.pbs.org.

30. Quoted in "The High Technology Way to Select a Baby's Sex."

31. Robert Wright, "Who Gets the Good Genes?" *Time,* January 11, 1999. www.time.com/time/magazine.

Chapter 3: The Promise and Perils of Information

32. Quoted in Anne Underwood, "A Certain Bittersweet Comfort," *Newsweek,* April 10, 2000, p. 60.

33. Quoted in Electronic Privacy Information Center, "Medical Record Privacy Home Page." www.epic.org/privacy/medical.

34. Lawrence O. Gostin, Zita Lazzarini, and Kathleen M. Flaherty, et al., "Legislative Survey of State Confidentiality Laws, with Specific Emphasis on HIV and Immunization," Washington, DC: 1997. www.epic.org/privacy/medical/cdc_survey.html.

35. Gostin, Lazzarini, and Flaherty, et al., "Legislative Survey of State Confidentiality Laws."

36. Testimony of Donna E. Shalala, Secretary, U.S. Department of Health and Human Services, before Senate Committee on Labor and Human Resources, September 11, 1997. aspe.os.dhhs.gov/admnsimp/pvctest.htm.

37. Quoted in Rick Weiss, "Discovery of 'Jewish' Cancer Gene Raises Fears of More than Disease," *Washington Post,* September 3, 1997, p. A3.

Chapter 4: Organ Transplants

38. Quoted in Susan Brody, "A Second Chance," *Contact Kids,* May 2000, p. 23.

39. Quoted in Rick Weiss, "New Rules for Organ Waiting Lists," *Washington Post,* March 27, 1998, p. A1.

40. Quoted in Arthur L. Caplan and Daniel H. Coelho, eds., *The Ethics of Organ Transplants.* Amherst, NY: Prometheus Books, 1998, pp. 287–88.

41. Quoted in Caplan and Coelho, eds., *The Ethics of Organ Transplants,* p. 177.

42. Quoted in Don Colburn, "Hey, Buddy, Can You Spare an Organ?" *Washington Post,* Health section, June 15, 1999, p. 18.

43. Jeffrey P. Kahn, "Take My Kidney, Please," *CNN Interactive,* January 11, 1998. www.cnn.com.

44. Quoted in Colburn, "Hey, Buddy, Can You Spare an Organ?" p. 21.

Chapter 5: Assisted Suicide

45. American Medical Association Home Page, "Current Opinions of the Council on Ethical and Judicial Affairs," E-2.211. www.ama-assn.org.

46. American Medical Association, "Current Opinions of the Council on Ethical and Judicial Affairs." E-2.211.

47. Testimony of Barbara Coombs Lee, before the Subcommittee on the Constitution, Committee on the Judiciary, U.S. House of Representatives, April 29, 1996. www.house.gov/judiciary/2173.htm.

48. American Medical Association, "Current Opinions of the Council on Ethical and Judicial Affairs." E-2.211.

49. Quoted in CNN transcript, "TalkBack Live: Should an Information Video on Euthanasia Be Shown on TV?" aired February 3, 2000. www.cnn.com.

50. Quoted in Joan Biskupic, "Unanimous Decision Points to Tradition of Valuing Life," *Washington Post,* June 27, 1997, p. A1.

51. Quoted in Biskupic, "Unanimous Decision Points to Tradition of Valuing Life."

52. Quoted in Amy Goldstein, "High Court's Decision on Suicides Leaves Doctors in a Gray Zone," *Washington Post,* June 27, 1997, p. A18.

53. Quoted in William Claiborne, "Kevorkian, Arguing Own Defense, Asks Jury to Disregard Law," *Washington Post,* March 26, 1999, p. A2.

54. Charles F. McKhann, *A Time to Die: The Place for Physician Assistance.* New Haven, CT: Yale University Press, 1999, p. 8.

55. McKhann, *A Time to Die,* pp. 188–89.

56. Quoted in William Claiborne, "'Death With Dignity' Fight May Make Oregon National Battleground," *Washington Post,* June 27, 1997, p. A19.

57. Quoted in *Barry Krischer v. Cecil McIver,* Supreme Court of Florida, Case No. 89,837, July 17, 1997. www.law.stetson.edu/elderlaw/krischer.htm.

58. Arthur L. Caplan, *Am I My Brother's Keeper? The Ethical Frontiers of Biomedicine.* Bloomington and Indianapolis: Indiana University Press, 1997, pp. 82–83.

59. Quoted in David Brown, "A Picture of Assisted Suicide," *Washington Post,* February 24, 2000, p. A3.

60. Quoted in Testimony of Barbara Coombs Lee, before the Subcommittee on the Constitution, Committee on the Judiciary, U.S. House of Representatives, April 29, 1996. www.house.gov/judiciary/2173.htm.

Glossary

Antibiotic: A substance derived from a microorganism used to treat disease.

Autonomy: Freedom to act independently and make one's own decisions.

Beneficence: Doing good, or performing helpful acts.

Bioethicist: One who analyzes and interprets medical ethics.

Cadaver organ: A body part, such as a kidney or liver, taken from the body of a person who recently died, for purposes of transplantation into another living person.

Chromosome: A unit of DNA, the inheritable matter found inside cells that relates to one's characteristics and functions. A normal human being has forty-six chromosomes, which are further divided into segments known as genes.

Common law: Legal rules based on court decisions and tradition (as opposed to enactments of legislatures).

Enzyme: A protein produced by cells that causes a chemical reaction in a body.

Ethicist: A person who analyzes and interprets ethical issues. Ethics are the principles and values that apply when people face moral issues, or questions of good and evil.

Euthanasia: Killing to end suffering.

Gene: Segment of chromosome that contains instructions for specific inheritable functions or processes.

Genetic engineering: The alteration of genetic material—DNA, genes, or chromosomes—to cause change in traits or functions.

Medical ethics: The principles and values that apply when people face questions of morality in medical care.

Mercy killing: Euthanasia.

Metabolism: The processing of substances by the body, often to break the substances down into elements that are useful to body functions.

Paradigm: Model or type, sometimes used to describe an approach to medical treatment.

Physician-assisted suicide: When a doctor helps a patient die, usually by providing lethal drugs and/or informing the patient about the amount of medication that will cause death.

Placebo: A substance that appears to be medication but that in fact has no medicinal effect. Placebos are used in experiments for purposes of comparison with a genuine medication or treatment.

Protocol: A detailed plan for a medical experiment.

Quarantine: Mandatory period of isolation to prevent the spread of disease.

Resuscitate: To revive from a near-death condition by, for example, restarting a person's heart or breathing.

Self-determination: The right to make decisions for oneself.

Terminal disease: An illness that results in death.

Toxin: Poison or impurity, often referred to in relation to substances produced by or introduced into the body.

Organizations
to Contact

The following organizations are concerned with medical ethics. The issues they address include organ transplants, assisted suicide and the right to die, and genetic engineering, as well as general ethical concerns relating to the field of medicine.

American Medical Association
515 N. State St.
Chicago, IL 60610
(312) 464-5000
Internet: www.ama-assn.org

The American Medical Association (AMA) is a three hundred thousand-member organization for physicians. In 1847, the AMA established a Code of Medical Ethics, which is continually revised and updated to take account of changing technologies and social values. The AMA's Council on Ethical and Judicial Affairs is a nine-member panel that interprets the Code of Medical Ethics and sets ethical policies for medical professionals. The AMA also has a separate Institute for Ethics, which is a research center that explores ethical issues facing doctors, patients, and the public.

Center for Bioethics, University of Pennsylvania
3401 Market St., Suite 320
Philadelphia, PA 19104-3308
(215) 898-7136
Internet: www.med.upenn.edu/bioethics/center

The Center for Bioethics, part of the University of Pennsylvania, is a private institution concerned with ethical, legal, social, and public policy issues in health care. Faculty members at the Center for Bioethics conduct research on such issues as genetic testing and engineering, experimental treatments, and organ transplants. The Center for Bioethics also sponsors *Bioethics.net,* an Internet resource that provides news, commentary, and analysis on a wide range of topics relating to medical ethics.

Hemlock Society
PO Box 101810
Denver, CO 80250-1810
(800) 247-7421
Internet: www.hemlock.org

The Hemlock Society supports the right of terminally ill individuals to choose to die and to have the assistance of a doctor to bring about death. It engages in efforts to pass laws in support of physician aid in dying, gets involved in court cases concerning the right to die and assisted suicide, and publishes materials on assisted suicide and related topics. The Hemlock Society describes itself as the oldest and largest right-to-die organization in the United States, with more than twenty-seven thousand members.

International Anti-Euthanasia Task Force
PO Box 760
Steubenville, OH 43952
(740) 282-3810
Internet: www.iaetf.org

The purpose of the International Anti-Euthanasia Task Force (IAETF) is to ensure that assisted suicide and euthanasia do not substitute for patients' rights to receive care. Toward this end, the IAETF produces research materials, supports lawyers who are involved in antieuthanasia work, and publishes a newsletter that provides current information on assisted suicide and euthanasia.

National Bioethics Advisory Commission
6705 Rockledge Drive, Suite 700
Rockville, MD 20892-7979
(301) 402-4242
Internet: www.bioethics.gov

The National Bioethics Advisory Commission (NBAC) was created by presidential order on October 3, 1995. The mission of this public organization is to provide advice and recommendations to the U.S. government on ethical issues arising from research into human biology and behavior. Toward this end, the NBAC holds public meetings around the country and publishes reports on medical, ethical, and policy issues.

National Coalition for Patient Rights
9 Bartlett St.
PMB 144
Andover, MA 01810-3883
(888) 44-PRIVACY
Internet: www.nationalcpr.org

The National Coalition for Patient Rights (CPR) is a nonprofit organization dedicated to the principle that patients have the right to privacy when they consult a health care professional and that the interests of employers, insurers, the government, and others should not interfere with that right. The National CPR presents testimony before Congress and other government bodies on health care confidentiality issues. The website contains news and information about privacy in medical care.

National Institutes of Health
9000 Rockville Pike
Bethesda, MD 20892
(301) 496-4000
Internet: www.nih.gov

Founded in 1887, the National Institutes of Health (NIH) is one of the world's leading centers for medical research. It has twenty-five separate institutes and centers, such as the

National Cancer Institute and the National Health, Lung, and Blood Institute. NIH states its mission as the acquisition of knowledge to help prevent, detect, diagnose, and treat disease and disability. It conducts research in its own laboratories and supports the research of other scientists in universities, medical schools, hospitals, and other institutions.

Office for Human Research Protections
U.S. Department of Health and Human Services
6100 Executive Blvd., Suite 3B01, MSC-7507
Rockville, MD 20892-7505
(301) 435-5646
Internet: http://ohrp.osophs.dhhs.gov

The Office for Human Research Protections (OHRP) is the U.S. government body that supervises government-funded research to ensure the protection of human (and animal) research subjects. The OHRP develops rules that researchers must follow to treat human research subjects ethically. The office also investigates allegations of unethical conduct in research and may take action to shut down experiments found to be too risky or otherwise ethically questionable.

United Network for Organ Sharing
1100 Boulders Pkwy., Suite 500
PO Box 13770
Richmond, VA 23225-8770
(888) TXINFO1
Internet: www.unos.org

The United Network for Organ Sharing (UNOS) maintains the U.S. organ transplant waiting list and brings together medical professionals, transplant recipients, and donor families to develop organ allocation policy under a contract with the U.S. Department of Health and Human Services. The organization also collects, analyzes, and publishes data on organ transplants.

Suggestions for Further Reading

Books

Catherine Baker, *Your Genes, Your Choices: Exploring the Issues Raised by Genetic Research*. Washington, DC: American Association for the Advancement of Science, 1999. (ehrweb.aaas.org/ehr/books/contents.html). This clearly written book describes the Human Genome Project. Using compelling real-life and hypothetical situations, the author thoughtfully presents the scientific underpinnings of the project, the goal of which is to identify and map the human genetic code, as well as the ethical, social, and legal issues that the project raises.

Lisa Belkin, *First Do No Harm*. New York: Simon & Schuster, 1993. Through the lives of real patients, their families, and their doctors, this book looks at life-and-death issues in medical ethics as they arose one summer at a city hospital in Texas. The inner workings of a hospital ethics committee are revealed, as doctors and others ponder the dilemmas posed by their patients. The author explores such issues as how far doctors should go to save a life, who decides such questions, and who pays.

Kathlyn Gay, *The Right to Die: Public Controversy, Private Matter*. Brookfield, CT: Milbrook Press, 1993. In easy-to-understand language, this book considers euthanasia, assisted suicide, and the right to die from ancient times to the present. In addition to airing both sides of the controversy as it plays out in the United States, the author also discusses the views and practices of other countries.

Jonathan D. Moreno, ed., *Arguing Euthanasia.* New York: Touchstone, 1995. In this collection of articles and essays, a variety of viewpoints are presented on euthanasia, assisted suicide, and the right to die. Contributors include such well-known commentators as Leon Kass, Nat Hentoff, and Ronald Dworkin.

Terry O'Neill, ed., *Biomedical Ethics: Opposing Viewpoints,* San Diego: Greenhaven Press, 1994. By presenting opposing viewpoints on the issues of medical testing, organ transplants, genetic technology, and human cloning, the author reveals the complexities of medical ethics.

Carol Wekesser, ed., *Genetic Engineering: Opposing Viewpoints.* San Diego: Greenhaven Press, 1996. This book includes articles from many different sources, presenting varied opinions on genetic engineering. Among the issues addressed are the safety or danger of genetic engineering, the pros and cons of genetic testing before birth, the options for regulating genetic engineering, and the benefits and harms of genetic therapy.

Lisa Yount, *Issues in Biomedical Ethics.* San Diego: Lucent Books, 1998. The author addresses the allocation of health care, physician-assisted suicide, the use of animals in medical research, and genetic engineering in this clearly written analysis of some of the pressing issues in medical ethics.

Websites

Bioethics.net, sponsored by the Center for Bioethics, University of Pennsylvania (www.bioethics.net). This wide-ranging yet user-friendly Internet resource offers medical ethics news, analysis, commentary, and links to numerous other online sites. Of particular interest to students are the site's detailed introductions to specific subjects, including genetics and assisted suicide, as well as a section entitled "Bioethics for Beginners."

Student Guide to the Human Genome Project, sponsored by the Department of Energy Office of Biological and Environmental Research (www.ornl.gov/hgmis/resource/

students.html). A variety of information and links to other sources of information make this Internet resource an excellent place to learn about genetics, genetic research, and the social, ethical, legal, and other issues raised by the Human Genome Project.

Works Consulted

Books

Arthur L. Caplan, *Am I My Brother's Keeper? The Ethical Frontiers of Biomedicine*. Bloomington and Indianapolis: Indiana University Press, 1997. A leading commentator on medical ethics addresses some of the most critical issues in the field, including medical testing, assisted suicide, organ transplantation, and genetic therapy.

Arthur L. Caplan and Daniel H. Coelho, eds., *The Ethics of Organ Transplants*. Amherst, NY: Prometheus Books, 1998. In this collection of articles, experts discuss the ethical issues posed by organ transplants, including the allocation of scarce organs, the use of organs from living donors, and payment for organs.

Bruce Hilton, *First Do No Harm: Wrestling with the New Medicine's Life & Death Dilemmas*. Nashville: Abingdon Press, 1991. Using examples drawn from actual events, the author explores a range of bioethical issues, from organ transplants to euthanasia to revamping the U.S. health care system.

Charles F. McKhann, *A Time to Die: The Place for Physician Assistance*. New Haven, CT: Yale University Press, 1999. The author, a professor of surgery at the Yale University School of Medicine, discusses the many sides of physician-assisted suicide and argues that it should be legally available in some circumstances. The author's discussions draw on his own experiences as a doctor and interviews with patients.

Plato, *The Republic of Plato*, Francis MacDonald Cornford, ed. and trans. New York: Oxford University Press, 1975.

Periodicals

Paul S. Appelbaum, "Threats to the Confidentiality of Medical Records: No Place to Hide," *Journal of the American Medical Association,* February 9, 2000.

Mark Asher, "The Inside Game," *Washington Post,* Health section, April 4, 2000.

Associated Press, "Distribution of Livers Will Be Revamped," *Washington Post,* March 14, 2000.

Associated Press, "Gore Urges Curbs on Genetic Testing," *Washington Post,* January 21, 1998.

Associated Press, "Wisconsin to Sue over New Transplant Policy, *Washington Post,* March 15, 2000.

A. L. Back, J. I. Wallace, H. E. Starks, and R. A. Pearlman, "Physician-Assisted Suicide and Euthanasia in Washington State," *Journal of the American Medical Association,* March 27, 1996.

Sharon Begley, "Decoding the Human Body," *Newsweek,* April 10, 2000.

Joan Biskupic, "Unanimous Decision Points to Tradition of Valuing Life," *Washington Post,* June 27, 1997.

Xavier Bosch, "Spain Leads World in Organ Donation and Transplantation," *Journal of the American Medical Association,* July 7, 1999.

Susan Brink, "Human Guinea Pigs," *U.S. News & World Report,* May 24, 1999.

―――, "Where Hope Never Dies," *U.S. News & World Report,* October 4, 1999.

Susan Brody, "A Second Chance," *Contact Kids,* May 2000.

David Brown, "A Picture of Assisted Suicide," *Washington Post,* February 24, 2000.

Shannon Brownlee and Sheila Kaplan, "High Risk, Without the Rewards," *U.S. News & World Report,* October 11, 1999.

Arthur L. Caplan, "With Transplants, Celebrity Can Help," *Breaking Bioethics,* February 3, 1999. www.bioethics.net.

Denise Casey, "What Can the New Gene Tests Tell Us?" *The Judges' Journal,* Summer 1997, updated October 1997.

William Claiborne, "'Death with Dignity' Fight May Make Oregon National Battleground," *Washington Post,* June 27, 1997.

———, "Kevorkian, Arguing Own Defense, Asks Jury to Disregard Law," *Washington Post,* March 26, 1999.

Don Colburn, "Hey, Buddy, Can You Spare an Organ?" *Washington Post,* Health section, June 15, 1999.

Geoffrey Cowley and Anne Underwood, "A Revolution in Medicine," *Newsweek,* April 10, 2000.

Juliet Eilperin, "House Acts to Reject Rules on Transplants, *Washington Post,* April 5, 2000.

Gary B. Ellis, "Keeping Research Subjects Out of Harm's Way," *Journal of the American Medical Association,* November 24, 1999.

———, "Protecting the Rights and Welfare of Human Research Subjects," *Academic Medicine,* September 1999.

"An Explanation of DNA, to the Letter," *Detroit Free Press,* October 19, 1999.

Alan Fleischman, "Medical Futility: How Much Is Too Much and Who Should Decide?" *Pediatric Ethicscope,* Spring & Summer 1998.

Frederic Golden, "Good Eggs, Bad Eggs," *Time,* January 11, 1999.

Amy Goldstein, "High Court's Decision on Suicides Leaves Doctors in a Gray Zone," *Washington Post,* June 27, 1997.

Avram Goldstein, "Kidney Donor Wants to Give Again," *Washington Post,* March 20, 2000.

Lawrence O. Gostin, Chai Feldblum, and David W. Webber, "Disability Discrimination in America: HIV/AIDS and Other Health Conditions," *Health Law and Ethics,* February 24, 1999.

Christopher Hallowell, "Playing the Odds: Health Insurers Want to Know What's in Your DNA," *Time,* January 11, 1999.

Dana Hawkins, "Dangerous Legacies: New Genetic Tests Provide Fresh Grounds for Discrimination," *U.S. News & World Report,* November 10, 1997.

James G. Hodge, Lawrence O. Gostin, and Peter D. Jacobson, "Legal Issues Concerning Electronic Health Information: Privacy, Quality, and Liability," *Health Law and Ethics,* October 20, 1999.

Walter Isaacson, "The Biotech Century," *Time,* January 11, 1999.

Leon Jaroff, "Fixing the Genes," *Time,* January 11, 1999.

———, "Success Stories," *Time,* January 11, 1999.

Jeffrey P. Kahn, "Take My Kidney, Please," *CNN Interactive,* January 11, 1998. www.cnn.com.

———, "When the Cure Seems Worse than the Disease," *CNN Interactive,* October 6, 1998. www.cnn.com.

Sheila Kaplan and Shannon Brownlee, "Duke's Hazards," *U.S. News & World Report,* May 24, 1999.

———, "Dying for a Cure," *U.S. News & World Report,* October 11, 1999.

Charles Krauthammer, "Yes, Let's Pay for Organs," *Time,* May 17, 1999.

Charlene Laino, "Technique Grows New Heart Vessels," *MSNBC,* November 9, 1998. www.msnbc.com.

"Legislation Sought Against Gene Bias," *Human Genome News,* January 1998. www.ornl.gov/hgmis/publicat/hgn/hgn.html.

Michael D. Lemonick, "Designer Babies," *Time,* January 11, 1999.

John P. Martin, "A World of Support: The Web Is Changing Medicine for Doctors and Patients, but Is This Leading to Better Health Care?" *Washington Post,* August 31, 1999.

Richard McCann, "To Whom It May Concern," *Washington Post,* March 5, 2000.

Usha Lee McFarling, "Locksmith of Our DNA," *Detroit Free Press,* October 19, 1999.

Usha Lee McFarling and Robert S. Boyd, "Who Are We? Science Nears an Answer," *Detroit Free Press,* October 19, 1999.

Glenn McGee, "Study Subject or Human Guinea Pig," *Breaking Bioethics,* December 10, 1998. www.bioethics.net.

———, "Tough Questions on 'Designer Babies,'" *Breaking Bioethics,* January 6, 1999. www.bioethics.net.

D. E. Meier, C. A. Emmons, S. Wallenstein, T. Quill, R. S. Morrison, and C. K. Cassel, "A National Survey of Physician-Assisted Suicide and Euthanasia in the United States," *New England Journal of Medicine,* April 23, 1998.

Terence Monmaney, "Gene Therapy Called Too Risky," *Los Angeles Times,* February 19, 2000.

Oliver Morton, "Overcoming Yuk," *Wired,* January 1998.

Arno G. Motulsky, "If I Had a Gene Test, What Would I Have and Who Would I Tell?" *Lancet,* July 24, 1999.

Deborah Nelson and Rick Weiss, "FDA Stops Researcher's Human Gene Therapy Experiments," *Washington Post,* March 2, 2000.

————, "Gene Test Deaths Not Reported Promptly," *Washington Post,* January 31, 2000.

————, "Hasty Decisions in the Race to a Cure?" *Washington Post*, November 21, 1999.

"New Round on Transplants," *Washington Post,* April 4, 2000.

Susan Okie, "Groups Warn of Breaches in Privacy Laws for Patients," *Washington Post,* April 16, 2000.

Richard Payne, "At the End of Life, Color Still Divides," *Washington Post,* Health section, February 15, 2000.

Pediatric Ethicscope, newsletter of the Office of Ethics, Children's Medical Center, Washington, DC.

Kristen Philipkoski, "Genome Map Only a Baby Step," *Wired,* March 28, 2000.

Neil D. Rosenberg, "Gene Therapy Grows Blood Vessels in Study," *Milwaukee Journal Sentinel,* November 10, 1998.

Rita Rubin, "Would I Gain by Being Tested? No," *U.S. News & World Report,* May 13, 1996.

Paul S. Russell, "Understanding Resource Use in Liver Transplantation," *Journal of the American Medical Association,* April 21, 1999.

Richard Saltus, "Beth Israel Halts Trial of Gene Therapy," *Boston Globe,* February 7, 2000.

Lindsey Austin Samahon, "Desperately Seeking a Cure," *U.S. News & World Report,* May 18, 1998.

John Schwartz, "Medical Web Sites Faulted on Privacy," *Washington Post,* February 1, 2000.

Joseph P. Shapiro, "Casting a Cold Eye on 'Death with Dignity,'" *U.S. News & World Report,* May 1, 1999.

John T. Sinnott and Sally H. Houston, "A Time to Die: The Place for Physician Assistance" (book review), *Journal of the American Medical Association,* January 26, 2000.

Wesley J. Smith, "Suicide Unlimited in Oregon," *The Weekly Standard,* November 8, 1999, reprinted in *IAETF Update,* October–December 1999. www.iaetf.org.

Roberto Suro, "States to Become Forum for Fight over Assisted Suicide," *Washington Post,* June 27, 1997.

Evan Thomas, "A Question of Privacy," *Newsweek,* November 8, 1999.

Anne Underwood, "A Certain Bittersweet Comfort," *Newsweek,* April 10, 2000.

Jill Waalen, "Genetic Testing Opens Brave New World," *Annals of Internal Medicine,* June 15, 1997.

LeRoy Walters, "Ethical Issues in Human Gene Therapy," *Human Genome News,* February 1999. www.ornl.gov/hgmis/publicat/hgn/hgn.html.

Tara Weingarten and Mark Hosenball, "A Fertile Scheme," *Newsweek,* November 8, 1999.

Rick Weiss, "Caution over Gene Therapy Puts Hopes on Hold," *Washington Post,* March 7, 2000.

———, "Discovery of 'Jewish' Cancer Gene Raises Fears of More than Disease," *Washington Post,* September 3, 1997.

———, "Embryo Work Raises Specter of Human Harvesting," *Washington Post,* June 14, 1999.

———, "Fertility Innovation or Exploitation?" *Washington Post*, February 9, 1998.

———, "For DNA, a Defining Moment," *Washington Post*, May 23, 2000.

———, "Gene Enhancements' Thorny Ethical Traits," *Washington Post*, October 12, 1997.

———, "Genetic Therapy Apparently Cures 2," *Washington Post*, April 28, 2000.

———, "Mighty Smart Mice," *Washington Post*, September 2, 1999.

———, "Monitoring Tightened for Genetic Research," *Washington Post*, March 8, 2000.

———, "New Rules for Organ Waiting Lists," *Washington Post*, March 27, 1998.

———, "Recruiting Foot Soldiers in HIV Siege," *Washington Post*, September 3, 1997.

———, "Transplant Researchers Clone 5 Pigs," *Washington Post*, March 15, 2000.

Rick Weiss and Justin Gillis, "DNA-Mapping Milestone Heralded," *Washington Post*, June 27, 2000.

Rick Weiss and Deborah Nelson, "Calls Grow for More Oversight of Gene Therapy," *Washington Post*, November 24, 1999.

———, "FDA Halts Experiments on Genes at University," *Washington Post*, January 22, 2000.

———, "Teen Dies Undergoing Experimental Gene Therapy," *Washington Post*, September 29, 1999.

———, "Victim's Dad Faults Gene Therapy Team," *Washington Post*, February 3, 2000.

Gregor Wolbring, "Eugenics, Euthenics, Euphenics," *GeneWatch*, a bulletin of the Council for Responsible

Genetics, June 1999. www.gene-watch.org/genewatch/
genejun.html.

Beverly Woodward, "Challenges to Human Subject
Protections in US Medical Research," *Journal of the
American Medical Association,* November 24, 1999.

Robert Wright, "Who Gets the Good Genes?" *Time,* January
11, 1999.

Internet Sources

American Medical Association, "Current Opinions of the
Council on Ethical and Judicial Affairs of the American
Medical Association," www.ama-assn.org.

Electronic Frontier Foundation, "Privacy—Medical and
Psychiatric Records and Drug Testing Archive."
www.eff.org/pub/Policy/Privacy/Medical.

Electronic Privacy Information Center, "Medical Record
Privacy Home Page." www.epic.org/privacy/medical.

Lawrence O. Gostin, Zita Lazzarini, and Kathleen M.
Flaherty, et al., "Legislative Survey of State Confidentiality
Laws, with Specific Emphasis on HIV and Immunization,"
1997. www.epic.org/privacy/medical/edc_survey.html.

Neil A. Holtzman and Michael S. Watson, eds., *Promoting
Safe and Effective Genetic Testing in the United States:
Final Report of the Task Force on Genetic Testing (a task
force of the U.S. National Institutes of Health-U.S.
Department of Energy Working Group on Ethical, Legal,
and Social Implications of Human Genome Research),*
September 1997. www.nhgri.nih.gov/ELSI/TFGI_final.

Barry Krischer v. Cecil McIver, Supreme Court of Florida,
Case No. 89,837, July 17, 1997.
www.law.stetson.edu/elderlaw/krischer.htm.

National Commission for the Protection of Human Subjects
of Biomedical and Behavioral Research, "Ethical Principles

and Guidelines for the Protection of Human Subjects of Research" (The Belmont Report), April 18, 1979. http://ohrp.osophs.dhhs.gov/humansubjects/guidance/belmont.htm.

PBS Online, "Cracking the Code," aired December 16, 1997, and "The Man-Made Man," aired December 23, 1997. www.pbs.org.

Testimony of Barbara Coombs Lee, before the Subcommittee on the Constitution, Committee on the Judiciary, U.S. House of Representatives, April 29, 1996. www.house.gov/judiciary/2173.htm.

Testimony of Donna E. Shalala, Secretary, U.S. Department of Health and Human Services, before Senate Committee on Labor and Human Resources, September 11, 1997. aspe.os.dhhs.gov/admnsimp/pvctest.htm.

U.S. Department of Labor, Department of Health and Human Services, Equal Employment Opportunity Commission, and Department of Justice, *Genetic Information and the Workplace*, January 20, 1998. www.nhgri.nih.gov/HGP/Reports/genetics_workplace.htm.

Websites

Hereditary Disease Foundation (www.hdfoundation.org). The foundation is a resource for people concerned with inherited, or genetic, diseases.

Human Genome News (www.ornl.gov/hgmis/publicat/hgn/hgn.html). This U.S. government-sponsored newsletter covers developments in the Human Genome Project.

Human Genome Project Information (www.ornl.gov/TechResources/Human-Genome). The Human Genome Project is the effort to map out and understand human DNA. This website, sponsored by the U.S. Department of Energy, provides information on many aspects of the project.

Kennedy Institute of Ethics, Georgetown University (www.georgetown.edu/research/kie). The institute conducts research and publishes material on a variety of ethical concerns, including medical ethics.

The National Human Genome Research Institute (www.nhgri.nih.gov). The institute represents the National Institutes of Health, the U.S. government's preeminent center for medical research, in the Human Genome Project.

National Institutes of Health—Bioethics Resources on the Web (www.nih.gov/sigs/bioethics/index.html). The National Institutes of Health provides links to various Internet resources relating to medical ethics.

Index

Picture Credits

Cover Photo: © Bob Daemmrich/Pictor
© AFP/Corbis, 43
© Peter G. Aitken/Photo Researchers, Inc., 14
AP Photo, 71
AP Photo/Eric Gay, 65
AP Photo/Alan Mothner, 69
© Ron Chapple/FPG International, 46
© Bettmann/Corbis, 15, 31
© Jacques M. Chenet/Corbis, 41
CNP/Archive Photos, 86
© FPG International, 81
© Owen Franken/Corbis, 53
© Grantpix/Photo Researchers, Inc., 89
© Vic Hinterlang/Impact Visuals, 7
© Kevin Laubacher/FPG International, 49
© Susie Leavines/Photo Researchers, Inc., 9
Library of Congress, 38
© Jose Luis Banus-March/FPG International, 35
© Will & Deni McIntyre/Photo Researchers, Inc., 52, 94
© Ryan McVay/PhotoDisc, 55
© Matt Meadows/Science Photo Library/Photo Researchers,
    Inc., 26
© Hank Morgan/Photo Researchers, Inc., 23
© John Moss/Science Source/Photo Researchers, Inc., 93
Crady Von Pawlak/Archive Photos, 47
© Photo Researchers, Inc., 20
© Doug Plummer/Photo Researchers, Inc., 13
© Vittoriano Rastelli/Corbis, 66, 75
© Roger Ressmeyer/Corbis, 19, 32
Reuters/Jonathan Drake/Archive Photos, 56
Reuters/John Hillery/Archive Photos, 90
Reuters/Mike Segar/Archive Photos, 61
© Bob Rowan; Progressive Image/Corbis, 59
© B. Seitz/Photo Researchers, Inc., 83
© Michael Simpson/FPG International, 29
© Adam Smith/FPG International, 39
Yad Vashem Photo Archives, courtesy of USHMM Photo
    Archives, 16

About the Author

Debbie Levy writes non-fiction, fiction, and poetry for adults and children. Her work on topics ranging from law to parenting to cyberspace has appeared in books, as well as in such publications as the *Washington Post, Legal Times, Washington Parent,* and *Highlights for Children.* Before turning to her writing career, Ms. Levy practiced law with a large Washington, D.C. law firm, and served as an editor for a national chain of newspapers for lawyers. She earned a B.A. in government and foreign affairs from the University of Virginia, and a J.D. and M.A. in politics from the University of Michigan. Ms. Levy enjoys kayaking and fishing in the Chesapeake Bay region, hiking just about anywhere, and playing the piano. She lives with her husband and their two sons in Chevy Chase, Maryland.